Behavioral Concepts in Manangement

Second Edition

BEHAVIORAL CONCEPTS IN MANAGEMENT

Second Edition

David R. Hampton

California State University,
San Diego

Dickenson Publishing Company, Inc.,
Encino, California, and Belmont, California

ISBN-0-8221-0081-9
Library of Congress Catalog Card Number: 72-81908

Printed in the United States of America

Printing (last digit): 9 8 7 6 5 4 3 2 1

For Davy

CONTENTS

PREFACE

The nature of management and behavior in organizations was not understood so well at the end of the 1950's as it is at the beginning of the 1970's. In large measure, this advance in understanding is due to the work of the men who are represented in this book. Many of them—McGregor, Herzberg, McClelland, Vroom, Lawler, Gellerman, Likert, Bennis, Argyris, and Blake and Mouton—are widely known for their contributions to creating and disseminating specific important uses of behavioral concepts in management. This book puts their work under one cover for convenient study.

The Introduction explains fully the particular way in which the book is organized. At this point I should like to thank the authors and publishers who allowed me to use the selections which appear in this volume. Without their generosity, this book could never have been produced.

I am also grateful to several people who reviewed the selections and my chapter introductions to them. I considered suggestions offered by Professor Edward J. Morrison of the University of Colorado, Professor Paul Hersey of Ohio University, Professor Daniel W. Geeding of Xavier University, and Professors Karl Price and Daryl Mitton of San Diego State College.

My wife Dorothy helped me with every stage of the book's preparation and freed me from many other chores which would have delayed the book or simply prevented its completion. I am deeply grateful to her.

DAVID R. HAMPTON
LA JOLLA, CALIFORNIA

xi

INTRODUCTION

The great strength of traditional administrative management theory was that it isolated and described some of the key levers by which the manager could influence the organization—the plans, the structures, the measurements and controls. The great weakness has proven to be that the relationships between moving the administrative levers and achieving organizational effectiveness were more tangled and obscured than had been believed. Theoretically sound organization hierarchies and patterns of task specialization brought success, but they brought side effects, too, in the form of conflict, apathy, and rigidity. Theoretically sound plans and controls had similarly mixed results. Clearly, formal organization arrangements and administrative practices were not the only strategic determinants of organizational behavior. There were forces at work in organizations which were not fully understood and which too often turned good intent to bad result.

The forces at work were people and groups of people. Human factors and social factors blend with administrative, organizational, technical, and economic inputs to shape human behavior in organization. But human and social factors were not very well understood by managers or taken into account by management theory. Much administrative action was designed in gross ignorance of how it would be perceived and responded to by people.

For the last half century, behavioral science research in industry has put administrative management theory and practice to the test. The results show that such practices as time and motion studies, wage incentives, budgets, efficiency controls, leadership styles, and divisions of labor are not simple and straightforward means of directing and controlling human behavior in organizations. Instead, they are stimuli which people and groups perceive and fit into

1

their own cognitive worlds. What motives and what behavior a new control or rule arouses depends as much upon human values and perceptions as upon the administrative device itself.

When he changes the boundaries and contents of jobs, when he changes the measurements and controls, when he installs new machines, even when he looks at employees, the manager sets in motion complex processes of perception, motivation, and behavior. His administrative actions ramify throughout the organization in unintended as well as intended ways.

Suppose, for example, that a supervisor tells his subordinates that he now wants to have the figures on expenses for the department every two weeks instead of every month, as in the past. Even if that's all the supervisor says, the subordinates may assume that expenses are now under closer scrutiny. They may act to make sure the figures look good when reported. In the process, the subordinates may choose to avoid certain expenditures which really ought to be made, but which would make the two-week expense figures exceed the budget. Perhaps all the supervisor had in mind was having data to put into a report for some other purpose, but his action to obtain that data triggered a chain of side effects.

These unintended results occur because the organization is a system, a set of interrelated and interdependent parts. The system includes human, social, administrative, organizational, technical, and economic factors. Since the parts are interdependent, the manager cannot touch one part without affecting the others. The work of behavioral scientists is to analyze the system and explain its interdependencies. Their particular contribution is increased knowledge of the human and social factors in organizational behavior. The payoff of their efforts for the manager can be an improved understanding of his world and better results in adapting his administrative actions to its realities.

For this payoff to be realized, however, the ever-increasing knowledge of the behavioral sciences must be transformed into managerial understanding and skill. Fortunately, an increasing number of behavioral scientists have focused on the problem. Selections from the works of some of the most stimulating and influential among them are pulled together for convenient study in this volume.

The selections are arranged to present a balance of conceptual and applied contributions, to exemplify two things: (1) representative basic ideas from the behavioral sciences which are now a part of contemporary thought in management, and (2) the use of these ideas in the full spectrum of management activities. Within each chapter the readings proceed from concept to application, from theory to practice. Thus, you will note an unusually strong continuity of thought within chapters.

Each of the first five chapters consists of a brief introduction and two or three articles. The first article offers a concise statement of the basic concepts of a particularly influential behavioral scientist. These articles also include some practical application of theory. The following articles in each chapter apply the concepts to management. In this way, you can examine the theories and policy recommendations of Douglas McGregor, Frederick Herzberg, Victor Vroom, Edward Lawler, III, David McClelland, and Rensis Likert, and see how Robert Golembiewski, M. Scott Myers, Robert Ford, Saul Gellerman, and Robert Stringer, Jr. put the theories to work to guide management practice.

There are a few slight variations from this basic pattern. In Chapter 4, both the first and second articles, by Vroom and Lawler, offer original concepts and apply them. Gellerman's closely related, applied article follows them. The second article in Chapter 5, by Weisbord, is an interview with the author of the first article, Rensis Likert, and one of his associates, David Bowers. This interview develops discussion of the practical uses of Likert's concepts.

The final chapter begins with a discussion by Warren Bennis of organization development and concludes with selections by Robert Blake and Jane Mouton on their technique, the managerial grid, for organizing and conducting efforts to improve management performance and by Chris Argyris on the use of T-groups for organizational effectiveness.

Although each of the major theorists and those writers who discuss the policy implications of their theories sees the organization as a system, each has a distinctive view of the system and would intervene at different points to make the system operate better. For McGregor, the starting point is gaining insight into the assumptions managers bring to their tasks and testing them against reality. For Herzberg, the key is the enrichment of jobs so that the work itself can better elicit a committed, enthusiastic performance. For McClelland (more precisely for Stringer), the critical opportunity is to reshape the control systems to make an organizational climate which will reinforce and reward achievement-oriented behavior. For Vroom and Lawler, changing the official system of monetary incentives is a neglected opportunity which can be better utilized. For Likert, a new approach to measuring organizational characteristics and human assets offers a new lever by which organizations can be moved to improved levels of performance. Finally, for Bennis, Blake and Mouton, and Argyris, intervention with laboratory education and other OD (organization development) techniques provides a method of planned organizational change.

My own experience in helping students and managers learn to use these systems of thought is that "The Gellerman Motivation and Productivity Film Series"[1] goes especially well with *Behavioral Concepts in Management.* When students and managers read McGregor, Herzberg, McClelland, Likert, Argyris, and Gellerman, then see these people and scenes depicting the behavior each is

[1] Each motion picture runs about twenty-five minutes. They are available from BNA Films, The Cineconference Center, 5615 Fishers Lane, Rockville, Maryland 20852.

concerned with, the students understand each system of thought even more clearly. So I suggest that the instructor use some or all of these films, if possible, to accompany the book.

The chapters and films can be paired as follows:

Chapter 1:   Human Nature and Management

Film: The Work of Douglas McGregor, Theory X and Theory Y—*Bennis, Beckard,* and *Jones*

Chapter 2:   Motivation-Hygiene Theory and Job Enrichment

Film: Motivation Through Job Enrichment—*Herzberg*

Chapter 3:   Achievement Motivation and Organizational Climate

Film: The Self-Motivated Achiever—*McClelland*

Chapter 4:   Rewards and Performance

Film: Understanding Motivation—*Gellerman*

Chapter 5:   Management Systems and the Human Organization

Film: The Mangement of Human Assets—*Likert*

Chapter 6:   Organization Development

Film: Human Nature and Organizational Realities—*Argyris*

For the most part, the authors who appear in the films set forth the same key ideas which they present in this volume. There are some variations, however. In his film, Gellerman discusses the general contribution of the behavioral sciences to management, whereas his article concentrates on the use of money to motivate. In his film, Argyris discusses the impact of organization on personality, the problems of interpersonal relationships among managers, and T-groups; in his article he concentrates on the latter two.

Suggested reading lists appear at the end of each chapter. For those who wish to pursue further study of the systems of thought presented in abbreviated fashion in this book, I have included books by each major theorist and have added a few sources by other authors. The lists are not meant to be exhaustive, but to suggest some useful directions for further reading.

The inclusion in this book of any particular scheme of thought does not, of course, suggest that you should (or that I do) accept it as predigested thinking. Naturally you do best by exercising your own critical intelligence in examining the ideas that follow. I must warn you that there are other concepts in management that do not fall within the scope of this book. To learn about them, you must read elsewhere. My intention is to introduce you to the important behavioral concepts in management. After reading and thinking about them, you may agree with George Strauss's description of some of this thinking (specifically the ideas of McGregor, Likert, and Bennis): "... despite their weaknesses, the theories in question are tremendously insightful and constitute the single best guide for management action that we have."[2]

To aid you in exercising your own critical intelligence, I have included in my introduction to each chapter a few questions. These questions are offered to help alert you to some of the central assumptions and ideas of the authors whose work you will read. After reading the articles, you might return to the questions and use them as a guide to assess your comprehension.

[2] George Strauss, "Human Relations—1968 Style," *Industrial Relations*, Vol. 7, No. 3 (May 1968), 276.

Chapter 1

HUMAN NATURE
AND MANAGEMENT

The first selection, Douglas McGregor's "The Human Side of Enterprise," could be called, without overstatement, the first and most provocative formulation of the new behavioral approach to management. In this landmark contribution to management education, McGregor reveals how managers are prisoners of their own assumptions, beliefs, or theories, whether or not they are conscious of them, and it is these ideas which form the mental picture of reality upon which managers premise their actions.

The manager's mental picture of human nature is particularly important. It provides the foundation upon which he erects his whole approach to management. If he sees man in general as inherently lazy, unintelligent, and inclined naturally to pursue goals contrary to the organization's interests, he will manage men accordingly. If he sees man as naturally inclined to work, naturally responsible, and sufficiently intelligent, he will manage according to that picture. In each case his assumptions about what people are like determine what his managerial practices will be.

McGregor describes the conventional picture of management's task and its supporting assumptions about human nature. He calls this Theory X. He contrasts Theory X with Theory Y, a picture of management's task based on a different set of beliefs about human nature. To provide a way of putting the theories to a test, he relates each approach, Theory X and Theory Y, to what behavioral scientists have learned and theorized about human needs. The results of this analysis shake the very foundations of some widespread patterns of management thought and open up some fresh alternative possibilities.

McGregor explains A. H. Maslow's hierarchy-of-needs concept, which depicts man's needs arranged in terms of levels of importance—from physiological and safety needs at the bottom, through social and ego needs, to self-fulfillment needs at the top. The Maslow theory of motivation holds that only unsatisfied needs motivate behavior. Offering a man what he already has or doesn't need will not motivate him. This is a simple idea, but its implications for management are not so widely and effectively utilized as they should be. McGregor encourages us to examine our own assumptions about people, how we think they are motivated, and, accordingly, what constitutes good management practice.

McGregor shows how a preoccupation with applying direction and control from above derives from a certain picture (Theory X) of human nature. He contrasts this approach with the emphasis on decentralization and delegation, job enlargement, participation and consultative management, and self-evaluation of performance—practices which derive from an alternative picture of people (Theory Y). To get the most out of McGregor, you need to question honestly your own assumptions about people and your ideas about effective management practices which derive from your assumptions. If you feel, after having read McGregor, that Theory Y is a soft approach, you need to read McGregor again. If you feel you like both Theory X and Theory Y and use both, you are saying that you favor mutually exclusive positions. You need to read McGregor again.

Within the general conceptual framework provided by McGregor, the article by Robert T. Golembiewski shows how the implicitly held management theories (X and Y) manifest themselves in contrasting managerial practice. Golembiewski demonstrates that the manner in which work is organized, planned, and controlled, and leadership and supervisory styles are patterned, depends upon the underlying theories of management, recognized or unrecognized. He also shows that alternative modes of organization, planning, control, and leadership have very different consequences, both in terms of human response and organizational effectiveness.

As you read this chapter, you may find it helpful to ask questions such as the following: What are the origins of the behavior called laziness or apathy, which we all see and have felt in business or school organizations? Are there any connections between the presence of this behavior and the impact of traditional management principles on personality? What evidence is there that the kind of theory these authors advocate leads to more effective management practice than the kind of theory they criticize? Are these articles consistent or inconsistent with texts with which I am familiar? What is my most recent employer's theory of human nature, and how does it manifest itself in managerial strategy? What is my own theory, and what are its implications?

The Human Side
of Enterprise

Douglas McGregor

It has become trite to say that the most significant developments of the next quarter century will take place not in the physical but in the social sciences, that industry—the economic organ of society—has the fundamental know-how to utilize physical science and technology for the material benefit of mankind, and that we must now learn how to utilize the social sciences to make our human organization truly effective.

Many people agree in principle with such statements; but so far they represent a pious hope—and little else. Consider with me, if you will, something of what may be involved when we attempt to transform the hope into reality.

I

Let me begin with an analogy. A quarter century ago basic conceptions of the nature of matter and energy had changed profoundly from what they had been since Newton's time. The physical scientists were persuaded that under proper conditions new and hitherto unimagined sources of energy could be made available to mankind.

We know what has happened since then. First came the bomb. Then, during the past decade, have come many other attempts to exploit these scientific discoveries—some successful, some not.

The point of my analogy, however, is that the application of theory in this field is a slow and costly matter. We expect it always to be thus. No one is impatient with the scientist because he cannot tell industry how to build a

Reprinted from *Leadership and Motivation* by Douglas McGregor, by permission of the M.I.T. Press, Cambridge, Massachusetts. Copyright © 1966 by The Massachusetts Institute of Technology.

simple, cheap, all-purpose source of atomic energy today. That it will take at least another decade and the investment of billions of dollars to achieve results which are economically competitive with present sources of power is understood and accepted.

It is transparently pretentious to suggest any *direct* similarity between the developments in the physical sciences leading to the harnessing of atomic energy and potential developments in the social sciences. Nevertheless, the analogy is not as absurd as it might appear to be at first glance.

To a lesser degree, and in a much more tentative fashion, we are in a position in the social sciences today like that of the physical sciences with respect to atomic energy in the thirites. We know that past conceptions of the nature of man are inadequate and in many ways incorrect. We are becoming quite certain that, under proper conditions, unimagined resources of creative human energy could become available within the organizational setting.

We cannot tell industrial management how to apply this new knowledge in simple, economic ways. We know it will require years of exploration, much costly development research, and a substantial amount of creative imagination on the part of management to discover how to apply this growing knowledge to the organization of human effort in industry.

May I ask that you keep this analogy in mind—overdrawn and pretentious though it may be—as a framework for what I have to say this morning.

Management's Task: Conventional View. The conventional conception of management's task in harnessing human energy to organizational requirements can be stated broadly in terms of three propositions. In order to avoid the complications introduced by a label, I shall call this set of propositions "Theory X":

> 1. Management is responsible for organizing the elements of productive enterprise—money, materials, equipment, people—in the interest of economic ends.
>
> 2. With respect to people, this is a process of directing their efforts, motivating them, controlling their actions, modifying their behavior to fit the needs of the organization.
>
> 3. Without this active intervention by management, people would be passive—even resistant—to organizational needs. They must therefore be persuaded, rewarded, punished, controlled—their activities must be directed. This is management's task—in managing subordinate managers or workers. We often sum it up by saying that management consists of getting things done through other people.

Behind this conventional theory there are several additional beliefs—less explicit, but widespread:

4. The average man is by nature indolent—he works as little as possible.

5. He lacks ambition, dislikes responsibility, prefers to be led.

6. He is inherently self-centered, indifferent to organizational needs.

7. He is by nature resistant to change.

8. He is gullible, not very bright, the ready dupe of the charlatan and the demagogue.

The human side of economic enterprise today is fashioned from propositions and beliefs such as these. Conventional organization structures, managerial policies, practices, and programs reflect these assumptions.

In accomplishing its task—with these assumptions as guides—management has conceived of a range of possibilities between two extremes.

The Hard or the Soft Approach?   At one extreme, management can be "hard" or "strong." The methods for directing behavior involve coercion and threat (usually disguised), close supervision, tight controls over behavior. At the other extreme, management can be "soft" or "weak." The methods for directing behavior involve being permissive, satisfying people's demands, achieving harmony. Then they will be tractable, accept direction.

This range has been fairly completely explored during the past half century, and management has learned some things from the exploration. There are difficulties in the "hard" approach. Force breeds counterforces: restriction of output, antagonism, militant unionism, subtle but effective sabotage of management objectives. This approach is especially difficult during times of full employment.

There are also difficulties in the "soft" approach. It leads frequently to the abdication of management—to harmony, perhaps, but to indifferent performance. People take advantage of the soft approach. They continually expect more, but they give less and less.

Currently, the popular theme is "firm but fair." This is an attempt to gain the advantages of both the hard and the soft approaches. It is reminiscent of Teddy Roosevelt's "speak softly and carry a big stick."

Is the Conventional View Correct?   The findings which are beginning to emerge from the social sciences challenge this whole set of beliefs about man and human nature and about the task of managment. The evidence is far from conclusive, certainly, but it is suggestive. It comes from the laboratory, the clinic, the schoolroom, the home, and even to a limited extent from industry itself.

The social scientist does not deny that human behavior in industrial organization today is approximately what management perceives it to be. He has, in fact, observed it and studied it fairly extensively. But he is pretty sure that this behavior is *not* a consequence of man's inherent nature. It is a consequence rather of the nature of industrial organizations, of management philosophy, policy, and practice. The conventional approach of Theory X is based on mistaken notions of what is cause and what is effect.

"Well," you ask, "what then is the *true* nature of man? What evidence leads the social scientist to deny what is obvious?" And, if I am not mistaken, you are also thinking, "Tell me—simply, and without a lot of scientific verbiage—what you think you know that is so unusual. Give me—without a lot of intellectual claptrap and theoretical nonsense—some practical ideas which will enable me to improve the situation in my organization. And remember, I'm faced with increasing costs and narrowing profit margins. I want proof that such ideas won't result simply in new and costly human relations frills. I want practical results, and I want them now."

If these are your wishes, you are going to be disappointed. Such requests can no more be met by the social scientist today than could comparable ones with respect to atomic energy be met by the physicist fifteen years ago. I can, however, indicate a few of the reasons for asserting that conventional assumptions about the human side of enterprise are inadequate. And I can suggest—tentatively—some of the propositions that will comprise a more adequate theory of the management of people. The magnitude of the task that confronts us will then, I think, be apparent.

II

Perhaps the best way to indicate why the conventional approach to management is inadequate is to consider the subject of motivation. In discussing this subject I will draw heavily on the work of my colleague, Abraham Maslow of Brandeis University. His is the most fruitful approach I know. Naturally, what I have to say will be overgeneralized and will ignore important qualifications. In the time at our disposal, this is inevitable.

Physiological and Safety Needs.   Man is a wanting animal—as soon as one of his needs is satisfied, another appears in its place. This process is unending. It continues from birth to death.

Man's needs are organized in a series of levels—a hierarchy of importance. At the lowest level, but preeminent in importance when they are thwarted, are his physiological needs. Man lives by bread alone, when there is no bread. Unless the circumstances are unusual, his needs for love, for status, for recognition are inoperative when his stomach has been empty for a while. But when he eats regularly and adequately, hunger ceases to be an important need. The sated man has hunger only in the sense that a full bottle has emptiness. The same is true of the other physiological needs of man—for rest, exercise, shelter, protection from the elements.

A satisfied need is not a motivator of behavior! This is a fact of profound significance. It is a fact which is regularly ignored in the conventional approach to the management of people. I shall return to it later. For the moment, one example will make my point. Consider your own need for air. Except as you are deprived of it, it has no appreciable motivating effect upon your behavior.

When the physiological needs are reasonably satisfied, needs at the next higher level begin to dominate man's behavior—to motivate him. These are called safety needs. They are needs for protection against danger, threat, deprivation. Some people mistakenly refer to these as needs for security. However, unless man is in a dependent relationship where he fears arbitrary deprivation, he does not demand security. The need is for the "fairest possible break." When he is confident of this, he is more than willing to take risks. But when he feels threatened or dependent, his greatest need is for guarantees, for protection, for security.

The fact needs little emphasis that since every industrial employee is in a dependent relationship, safety needs may assume considerable importance. Arbitrary management actions, behavior which arouses uncertainty with respect to continued employment or which reflects favoritism or discrimination, unpredictable administration of policy—these can be powerful motivators of the safety needs in the employment relationship *at every level* from worker to vice president.

Social Needs.   When man's physiological needs are satisfied and he is no longer fearful about his physical welfare, his social needs become important motivators of his behavior—for belonging, for association, for acceptance by his fellows, for giving and receiving friendship and love.

Management knows today of the existence of these needs, but it often assumes quite wrongly that they represent a threat to the organization. Many studies have demonstrated that the tightly knit, cohesive work group may, under proper conditions, be far more effective than an equal number of separate individuals in achieving organizational goals.

Yet management, fearing group hostility to its own objectives, often goes to considerable lengths to control and direct human efforts in ways that are inimical to the natural "groupiness" of human beings. When man's social needs—and perhaps his safety needs, too—are thus thwarted, he behaves in ways which tend to defeat organizational objectives. He becomes resistant, antagonistic, uncooperative. But this behavior is a consequence, not a cause.

Ego Needs.   Above the social needs—in the sense that they do not become motivators until lower needs are reasonably satisfied—are the needs of greatest signficance to management and to man himself. They are the egoistic needs, and they are of two kinds:

1. Those needs that relate to one's self-esteem—needs for self-confidence, for independence, for achievement, for competence, for knowledge.

2. Those needs that relate to one's reputation—needs for status, for recognition, for appreciation, for the deserved respect of one's fellows.

Unlike the lower needs, these are rarely satisfied; man seeks indefinitely for more satisfaction of these needs once they have become important to him. But they do not appear in any significant way until physiological, safety, and social needs are all reasonably satisfied.

The typical industrial organization offers few opportunities for the satisfaction of these egoistic needs to people at lower levels in the hierarchy. The conventional methods of organizing work, particularly in mass production industries, give little heed to these aspects of human motivation. If the practices of scientific management were deliberately calculated to thwart these needs—which, of course, they are not—they could hardly accomplish this purpose better than they do.

Self-fulfillment Needs.   Finally—a capstone, as it were, on the hierarchy of man's needs—there are what we may call the needs for self-fulfillment. These are the needs for realizing one's own potentialities, for continued self-development, for being creative in the broadest sense of that term.

It is clear that the conditions of modern life give only limited opportunity for these relatively weak needs to obtain expression. The deprivation most people experience with respect to their lower-level needs diverts their energies into the struggle to satisfy *those* needs, and the needs for self-fulfillment remain dormant.

III

Now, briefly, a few general comments about motivation:

We recognize readily enough that a man suffering from a severe dietary deficiency is sick. The deprivation of physiological needs has behavioral consequences. The same is true—although less well recognized—of deprivation of higher-level needs. The man whose needs for safety, association, independence, or status are thwarted is sick just as surely as is he who has rickets. And his sickness will have behavioral consequences. We will be mistaken if we attribute his resultant passivity, his hostility, his refusal to accept responsibility to his inherent "human nature." These forms of behavior are *symptoms* of illness—of deprivation of his social and egoistic needs.

The man whose lower-level needs are satisfied is not motivated to satisfy those needs any longer. For practical purposes they exist no longer. (Remember my point about your need for air.) Management often asks, "Why aren't people more productive? We pay good wages, provide good working conditions, have excellent fringe benefits and steady employment. Yet people do not seem to be willing to put forth more than minimum effort."

The fact that management has provided for these physiological and safety needs has shifted the motivational emphasis to the social and perhaps to the egoistic needs. Unless there are opportunities *at work* to satisfy these higher-level needs, people will be deprived; and their behavior will reflect this deprivation. Under such conditions, if management continues to focus its attention on physiological needs, its efforts are bound to be ineffective.

People *will* make insistent demands for more money under these conditions. It becomes more important than ever to buy the material goods and services which can provide limited satisfaction of the thwarted needs. Although money has only limited value in satisfying many higher-level needs, it can become the focus of interest if it is the *only* means available.

The Carrot and Stick Approach. The carrot and stick theory of motivation (like Newtonian physical theory) works reasonably well under certain circumstances. The *means* for satisfying man's physiological and (within limits) his safety needs can be provided or withheld by management. Employment itself is such a means, and so are wages, working conditions, and benefits. By these means the individual can be controlled so long as he is struggling for subsistence. Man lives for bread alone when there is no bread.

But the carrot and stick theory does not work at all once man has reached an adequate subsistence level and is motivated primarily by higher needs. Management cannot provide a man with self-respect, or with the respect of his fellows, or with the satisfaction of needs for self-fulfillment. It can create conditions such that he is encouraged and enabled to seek such satisfactions *for himself*, or it can thwart him by failing to create those conditions.

But this creation of conditions is not "control." It is not a good device for directing behavior. And so management finds itself in an odd position. The high standard of living created by our modern technological know-how provides quite adequately for the satisfaction of physiological and safety needs. The only significant exception is where management practices have not created confidence in a "fair break"—and thus where safety needs are thwarted. But by making possible the satisfaction of low-level needs, management has deprived itself of the ability to use as motivators the devices on which conventional theory has taught it to rely—rewards, promises, incentives, or threats and other coercive devices.

Neither Hard nor Soft. The philosophy of management by direction and control—*regardless of whether it is hard or soft*—is inadequate to motivate because the human needs on which this approach relies are today unimportant motivators of behavior. Direction and control are essentially useless in motivating people whose important needs are social and egoistic. Both the hard and the soft approach fail today because they are simply irrelevant to the situation.

People, deprived of opportunities to satisfy at work the needs which are now important to them, behave exactly as we might predict—with indolence, passivity, resistance to change, lack of responsibility, willingness to follow the demagogue, unreasonable demands for economic benefits. It would seem that we are caught in a web of our own weaving.

In summary, then, of these comments about motivation:

Management by direction and control—whether implemented with the hard, the soft, or the firm but fair approach—fails under today's conditions to provide effective motivation of human effort toward organizational objectives. It fails because direction and control are useless methods of motivating people whose physiological and safety needs are reasonably satisfied and whose social, egoistic, and self-fulfillment needs are predominant.

IV

For these and many other reasons, we require a different theory of the task of managing people based on more adequate assumptions about human nature and human motivation. I am going to be so bold as to suggest the broad dimensions of such a theory. Call it "Theory Y," if you will.

1. Management is responsible for organizing the elements of productive enterprise—money, materials, equipment, people—in the interest of economic ends.

2. People are *not* by nature passive or resistant to organizational needs. They have become so as a result of experience in organizations.

3. The motivation, the potential for development, the capacity for assuming responsibility, and readiness to direct behavior toward organizational goals are all present in people. Management does not put them there. It is a responsibility of management to make it possible for people to recognize and develop these human characteristics for themselves.

4. The essential task of management is to arrange organizational conditions and methods of operation so that people can achieve their own goals *best* by directing *their own* efforts toward organizational objectives.

This is a process primarily of creating opportunities, releasing potential, removing obstacles, encouraging growth, providing guidance. It is what Peter Drucker has called "management by objectives" in contrast to "management by control."

And I hasten to add that it does *not* involve the abdication of management, the absence of leadership, the lowering of standards, or the other characteristics usually associated with the "soft" approach under Theory X. Much on the contrary. It is no more possible to create an organization today which will be a fully effective application of this theory than it was to build an atomic power plant in 1945. There are many formidable obstacles to overcome.

Some Difficulties. The conditions imposed by conventional organization theory and by the approach of scientific management for the past half century have tied men to limited jobs which do not utilize their capabilities, have discouraged the acceptance of responsibility, have encouraged passivity, have eliminated meaning from work. Man's habits, attitudes, expectations—his whole conception of membership in an industrial organization—have been conditioned by his experience under these circumstances. Change in the direction of Theory Y will be slow, and it will require extensive modification of the attitudes of management and workers alike.

People today are accustomed to being directed, manipulated, controlled in industrial organizations and to finding satisfaction for their social, egoistic, and self-fulfillment needs away from the job. This is true of much of management as well as of workers. Genuine "industrial citizenship"—to borrow again a term from Drucker—is a remote and unrealistic idea, the meaning of which has not even been considered by most members of industrial organizations.

Another way of saying this is that Theory X places exclusive reliance upon external control of human behavior, while Theory Y relies heavily on self-control and self-direction. It is worth noting that this difference is the difference between treating people as children and treating them as mature adults. After generations of the former, we cannot expect to shift to the latter overnight.

V

Before we are overwhelmed by the obstacles, let us remember that the application of theory is always slow. Progress is usually achieved in small steps.

Consider with me a few innovative ideas which are entirely consistent with Theory Y and which are today being applied with some success:

Decentralization and Delegation. These are ways of freeing people from the too-close control of conventional organization, giving them a degree of freedom to direct their own activities, to assume responsibility, and, importantly, to satisfy their egoistic needs. In this connection, the flat organization of Sears, Roebuck and Company provides an interesting example. It forces "managment by objectives" since it enlarges the number of people reporting to a manager until he cannot direct and control them in the conventional manner.

Job Enlargement.   This concept, pioneered by IBM and Detroit Edison, is quite consistent with Theory Y. It encourages the acceptance of responsibility at the bottom of the organization; it provides opportunities for satisfying social and egoistic needs. In fact, the reorganization of work at the factory level offers one of the more challenging opportunities for innovation consistent with Theory Y. The studies by A.T.M. Wilson and his associates of British coal mining and Indian textile manufacture have added appreciably to our understanding of work organization. Moreover, the economic and psychological results achieved by this work have been substantial.

Participation and Consultative Management.   Under proper conditions these results provide encouragement to people to direct their creative energies toward organizational objectives, give them some voice in decisions that affect them, provide significant opportunities for the satisfaction of social and egoistic needs. I need only mention the Scanlon Plan as the outstanding embodiment of these ideas in practice.

The not infrequent failure of such ideas as these to work as well as expected is often attributable to the fact that a management has "bought the idea" but applied it within the framework of Theory X and its assumptions.

Delegation is not an effective way of exercising management by control. Participation becomes a farce when it is applied as a sales gimmick or a device for kidding people into thinking they are important. Only the management that has confidence in human capacities and is itself directed toward organizational objectives rather than toward the preservation of personal power can grasp the implications of this emerging theory. Such management will find and apply successfully other innovative ideas as we move slowly toward the full implementation of a theory like Y.

Performance Appraisal.   Before I stop, let me mention one other practical application of Theory Y which—while still highly tentative—may well have important consequences. This has to do with performance appraisal within the ranks of management. Even a cursory examination of conventional programs of performance appraisal will reveal how completely consistent they are with Theory X. In fact, most such programs tend to treat the individual as though he were a product under inspection on the assembly line.

Take the typical plan: substitute "product" for "subordinate being appraised," substitute "inspector" for "superior making the appraisal," substitute "rework" for "training or development," and, except for the attributes being judged, the human appraisal process will be virtually indistinguishable from the product inspection process.

A few companies—among them General Mills, Ansul Chemical, and General Electric—have been experimenting with approaches which involve the individual in setting "targets" or objectives *for himself* and in a *self*-evaluation of performance semi-annually or annually. Of course, the superior plays an important leadership role in this process—one, in fact, which demands substantially more competence than the conventional approach. The role is, however, considerably more congenial to many managers than the role of "judge" or "inspector" which is forced upon them by conventional performance. Above all, the individual is encouraged to take a greater responsibility for planning and appraising his own contribution to organizational objectives; and the accompanying effects on egoistic and self-fulfillment needs are substantial. This approach to performance appraisal represents one more innovative idea being explored by a few managements who are moving toward the implementation of Theory Y.

VI

And now I am back where I began. I share the belief that we could realize substantial improvements in the effectiveness of industrial organizations during the next decade or two. Moreover, I believe the social sciences can contribute much to such developments. We are only beginning to grasp the implications of the growing body of knowledge in these fields. But if this conviction is to become a reality instead of a pious hope, we will need to view the process much as we view the process of releasing the energy of the atom for constructive human ends—as a slow, costly, sometimes discouraging approach toward a goal which would seem to many to be quite unrealistic.

The ingenuity and the perseverance of industrial management in the pursuit of economic ends have changed many scientific and technological dreams into commonplace realities. It is now becoming clear that the application of these same talents to the human side of enterprise will not only enhance substanitally these materialistic achievements but will bring us one step closer to "the good society." Shall we get on with the job?

Organizing Work:
Theories and
Techniques

Robert T. Golembiewski

Notions about the act of organizing are changing drastically. At one time, what may be called Taylorian techniques dominated thought about organizing. They ranged from time-and-methods study to the statistical determination of "standard times," all in the tradition of the work of Frederick W. Taylor.

These techniques permitted a new view of the management problems. Directly, the techniques often were employed in designing individual tasks. Indirectly, the implicit theory underlying the techniques guided organizing at all levels.

Increasingly, however, two propositions are moving to center stage: (1) that any technique depends upon an explicit theory of when and how it is to be applied; (2) and that there is nothing so practical as a good theory, nothing so costly as an inadequate one.

The stake the manager has in this changing concept may be spotlighted by considering the question: Which of two theories is more useful for guiding applications of Taylorian techniques at all levels of an industrial or administrative organization? The effort may seem curious, for Taylorian techniques often have been used to organize work as if there were a "one best way." Taylor himself would have none of this approach, but many followers have not taken him at his word!

The importance of theory is often underplayed. Indeed, theory is usually thought of as the direct opposite of action, as speculative and impractical. This is true of bad theories. A good theory, however, provides a picture of what is related to what. This knowledge is indispensable both for describing what exists and for prescribing how desired objectives can be attained.

Reprinted from *Advanced Management—Office Executive*, Vol. I, No. 6 (June, 1962), 26-30, by permission of the author and the Society for Advancement of Management.

The failures of applications of Taylorian techniques sharply demonstrate the importance of theory. Many of these failures have been reported,[1] and they underscore the importance of knowing which techniques work under which conditions. A good theory gives this information.

Applications of Taylorian techniques tend to be guided by an underlying theory, "Theory X."[2] For example, the left-hand column in Figure 1 lists the prepositions of Theory X which are commonly made explicit. The right-hand column lists major unarticulated propositions *implied* by Theory X.

Theory X holds that efficiency will be high when:	Theory X assumes that:
1. Authority flows in a single stream from organization superiors to subordinates.	1'. Work is inherently distasteful to most people.
2. Supervision is detailed and the span of control is narrow.	2'. Most people prefer to be directed, and have little desire for responsibility and little ambition.
3. The individual is considered to be a social isolate and his physiological properties are respected in organizing work.	3. Most people have little capacity for creativity in solving organization problems.
4. Work is routinized.	4'. Motivation occurs only at a bread-and-butter level.
	5'. Most people must be closely controlled and often coerced to achieve organization objectives.

Figure 1.

There may be protests. Few individuals would deny that the propositions in the left-hand column—the "principles of organization" familiar to even the least-conscientious reader of the literature—have been at the center of thought about organizing. Many may question those in the right-hand column. However, such views seem common among managers.[3]

In any case, the properties in the left-hand column must be based on propositions like those on the right. Try, for example, changing 1'. to read: "Work is natural to man." This substitution will provide no support for principles of organization such as detailed supervision. The example is not rigged. Variations of this game in logic will yield a similar result.

Another theory, "Theory Y,"[2] could underlie applications of Taylorian techniques. Theory Y may be outlined as shown in Figure 2.

Theory Y, patently, contrasts sharply with Theory X. The contrast of theories, however, does not establish Theory Y's claim to guide Taylorian applications. Hence the focus below on this crucial question: Will Theory X or Theory Y be more effective in guiding applications of Taylorian techniques?

The analysis will show that the sparse use of Theory Y has been unfortunate. This is not to say that Theory Y is always more effective, for both theories will be useful in certain cases. However, if a manager were to bet, he will be well advised to choose Theory Y as more likely to guide effective applications.

Theory Y holds that efficiency will be high when:	Theory Y assumes that:
1. Authority flows from formal and informal sources—up, down, and across the organization—which are oriented in the same direction.	1′. Work is as natural as play, if the conditions are favorable.
2. Supervision is general and the span of control is wide.	2′. Self-control is often indispensable in achieving organization goals.
3. The individual can behave as a social and psychological being—as well as a physiological being—that is, when work does not ignore the fullness of man.	3′. Self-control in line with organization objectives is a function of rewards which satisfy ego and social needs, as well as bread-and-butter needs.
4. The task is a meaningful whole, providing some variety and requiring some skill and judgment.	4′. The capacity for creativity in solving organizational problems is widely distributed in the population.
	5′. This capacity for creativity is under-utilized in organizations.

Figure 2.

Four major points of comparison between Theory X and Theory Y will be emphasized here: routinization; social isolation; span of control; and style of supervision.

Routinization is not inherent in applications of Taylorian techniques. Consider this simple distinction: Work may be highly engineered; and highly engineered work may be routinized; but not all highly engineered work is routinized. For example, some of the most highly engineered tasks—those of the surgeon or the pilot—are hardly routinized.

Routinization, then, derives from theory rather than technique. Techniques may isolate the basic operations of a task and their sequence, let us say, o_1, o_2, and o_3. Theory X and Theory Y (see especially proposition 4 in each) yield two degrees of routinization when the operations are organized as in Figures 3 and 4.

Employee A	Employee B	Employee C
↓	↓	↓
o_1	o_2	o_3 → Product

Figure 3.   *Theory X and organizing a task.*

Research treats Theory X poorly, while it demonstrates the payoffs of Theory Y's attempt to involve the individual in his work or reduce boredom. In short, work must give to get. Not that work ought to be, or can be, organized to require the counterparts of surgeons or pilots. Even humble approaches to Theory Y often will pay off handsomely.

Employee A $\rightarrow o_1 + o_2 + o_3 \rightarrow$ Product
Employee B $\rightarrow o_1 + o_2 + o_3 \rightarrow$ Product
Employee C $\rightarrow o_1 + o_2 + o_3 \rightarrow$ Product

Figure 4. *Theory Y and organizing a task.*

Consider an example drawn from the administration of paper.[4] Originally, Theory X guided the processing of mail in a mail-order house. Thus each clerk handled only letters which could be answered by printed form letter. The few letters which required unprogrammed attention would be passed on to a supervisor. In addition, each clerk handled but a single type of letter, such as complaint letters or inquiries. That is, the work was routinized as well as engineered.

Theory Y was approached simply in a reorganization. The work was engineered as fully as before, but it was less routinized. Each clerk handled all thirty-nine types of letters involved in routine relations with, for example, all customers whose names began with A, and each clerk made suggestions to her supervisor as to the handling of rare communications which cannot be answered by form letter. The reorganization had startling effects. Productivity increased almost 30 per cent, and personnel turnover dropped by 66 per cent.

The technique of job enlargement is given much lip service. Thus no claim for discovery is being made here. Rather the point is three-fold. First, the success of job enlargement implies the need to scrutinize Theory X very closely. Second, much work in organizations is over-routinized. Granted that at early stages of technological development, routinization may be necessary, there appear to be rather narrow limits beyond which the costs of routinization may be said to overbalance returns. When these limits are passed, Theory Y becomes a necessary emphasis.

CAN PAY BIG RETURNS IN OUTPUT

Third, substantial reorganization of work is not always necessary to derive benefits from Theory Y. Training in, or rotation through, a number of routine tasks, for example, can pay big returns in output and satisfaction.

Theory X emphasizes the individual as a neurophysiological being who responds consistently to the formal organization as his sole authoritative source. Also, the individual is regarded as a social isolate. These naked positions seem patently false, which they are, but they often influence managerial behavior because they are logically consistent with Theory X.

To illustrate, Theory X holds that authority is one-way, a view which logically requires the assumption that the individual is a physiological and isolated being. In contrast, if the individual is acknowledged to have social ties, a cross-

...ure condition exists. That is, the individual must meet conflicting demands ...ization and from his group ties. This cross-pressure condition, of ...at authority is a one-line relation.

...ys a high price for logical consistency. Experiments with group ... for example, reveal the power of the informal group in con-... Figure 5 compares the exhortation by management of all ...ase productivity (consistent with Theory X) with the attempt ... norm supporting high output among a few operatives (consis-... .[5]

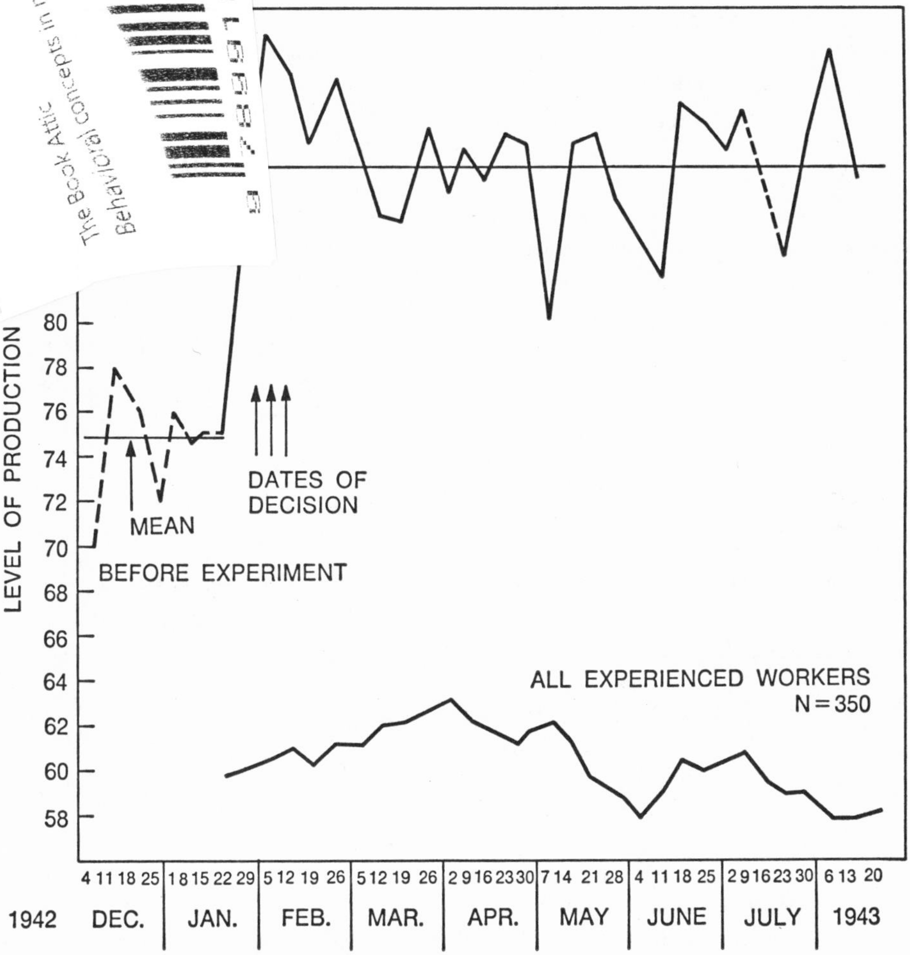

Figure 5. *The effects of "group decision-making" (upper curve) versus management exhortation (lower curve) in increasing output.*

The lower curve mutely testifies that the neglect of man's social relations by Theory X often has little to recommend it. This conclusion holds for any level of the organization.

SOME MEASURE OF ADVANTAGE

Significantly, also, the job in question had been "set" by time-and-motion studies. The number of units considered "standard" was 60, and the physical maximum for the job was 75. The increase in average output for the workers who made group decisions—from 75 to 87 units per day—is some measure of Theory Y's advantage in motivating employees. Of course, even 75 units probably could not have been achieved if the job had not been engineered with the help of Taylorian techniques.

It is often surprising how easily Theory Y can be approached and how rewarding the effort can be, considering the delicacy and complexity of dealing with the group relations which I have analyzed in detail elsewhere.[6] Consider the simple technique of allowing work teams to choose their own members. The technique recognizes man's dependence upon his social relations in a vital way. Above-choice, in contrast, respects one-line authority and is thus consistent with Theory X. Theory X, again, comes out second-best.

On a construction project, self-choice teams proved more effective on four measures: job satisfaction; turnover rate; an index of labor cost; and an index of materials cost. In terms of labor cost alone, for example, the self-choice crews produced four houses per 100 more than above-choice teams.[7]

WELL TO BE GUIDED BY THEORY Y

Taylorian techniques, then, would do well to be guided by Theory Y. The multiplicity of authoritative sources, formal and informal, to which individuals respond is a fact of life in organizations. The basic goal is to tie these sources together so that they are oriented in a common direction. This approach makes the best of the diversity of authoritative sources.

Theory X, in contrast, neglects the individual in his social fullness. This neglect precipitates problems, as well as overlooks significant sources of control. Thus adherence to Theory X in reorganizing pays the price of inducing resistance because of the failure to take existing group relations into account.[8]

Theory X prescribes a narrow span of control. The "three and seven" rule, for example, exemplifies traditional thinking. This rule holds that, wherever possible, no fewer than three and no more than seven employees should report to any single supervisor. Theory Y, in contrast, prescribes a much broader span of control.

The two structures generated by Theory X and Theory Y have particularly important consequences for four features of administration at all levels: "power"; training; communication; and the scope of jobs. In a hypothetical organization structure generated by Theory X, suppose we have 18 supervisors (S) under one manager (M).

"Power"—in general, the measure of the degree to which a supervisor actually controls his immediate work environment—cannot be neglected in organizing. Of course, all supervisors at the same level have the same formal authority, but not all supervisors have equal power. The supervisor with high power, research reveals, tends to be the effective supervisor.[9] Thus high-power supervisors tend to have high-output work units.

These findings are reasonable. For a relatively powerless supervisor is merely a glorified middle man who transmits orders from above. Therefore he is not often capable of motivating his employees. He is a pathetic figure in a web not of his choosing.

Theory X implies substantial costs due to lower supervisory "power." Consider two supervisors, S_x and S_y. Assume that a similar decision is to be made in the two structures. The Theory X structure would tend to lower supervisory power. For M_x (the manager) would tend to exercise close control over the decision-making of S_x. Indeed, M_x might demand to make many decisions, even in relatively trifling matters. Certainly it would be easy for M_x to define his role in this way. But convenience has its price—a time-lag in decision-making and a demonstration to one and all that S_x had relatively little power.

The Theory Y structure, in contrast, would increase supervisory power. Indeed, the problem in this structure is to force major problems up to the level of M_y. M_y would have to train his supervisors to take action. M_y simply could not behave like M_x: he would spread himself too thin.

Further, the two organization forms also substantially influence the degree to which a job serves as a training ground for the employee. M_y, it is true, might foster some loss of efficiency by training his subordinates to act. For M_y might be able to make decisions of a higher quality.

LESS EQUIPPED TO MOVE UP

But more ambitious and able personnel want a test. Moreover, in the long run, one learns best from one's own mistakes. M_x does not present his subordinates with the same challenge or opportunity to learn. Consequently, the subordinates of M_x would be less equipped to move up to greater responsibility.

Also, these subordinates would be likely to include a higher percentage of untested deadwood than M_y's batch.

Experience in Sears, Roebuck's medium-size stores, for example, supports this position.[10] These stores were organized as either Theory X or Theory Y prescribe. The Theory X stores had lower satisfaction. And besides, Theory X stores contributed much less than their share of supervisors who were considered as capable candidates for promotion.

In addition, the two organization forms have important effects on communication. Thus Theory X organizations have more levels than Theory Y organizations, given equal numbers of personnel. The more levels, of course, the greater the probability of having distorted (or "noisy") communication.

Obviously, three levels of organization require one more communication link upwards than two levels. Moreover, as you add levels—and thus increase social distance—what gets communicated upward tends to change.[11] The greater the perceived social distance between individuals, the greater the tendency to communicate favorable things upward. This "sweetening" is often pronounced.

Finally, Theory X discourages lateral communication. That is, it encourages communication up and over and back again rather than across. By contrast, when getting the job done in Theory Y structures, lateral communication is indispensable for solving the supervisory jurisdictional issues which the head man has encouraged the supervisors to settle whenever possible.

The communication costs of Theory X may be great. Consider only lateral communication. Theory X discourages problem-solving at the level which often has the relevant information and knowledge. The "power" of heads of subordinate units thereby suffers. In addition, the proliferation of staff is a normal concomitant of the top man attempting to do what his subordinates are paid for doing. Such growth does not always solve problems of communication and control.

Finally, unless the head man is affirmative about encouraging lateral communication, he will often be forced to fight many fires. Firefighting does not mix well, say, with long-range planning or with cultivating the organization image, both of which often will go by default without top-level guidance. Nor is the training of subordinates encouraged by the temperament suitable to a Great Firefighter.

The two organization structures just described also affect the scope of jobs and, thereby, significantly influence the development and monitoring of measures of performance. The task, surprisingly, is often easier for jobs with some scope (Theory Y) than for highly routinized jobs (Theory X).

For example, given a Theory X job, at least three checks would be necessary to monitor work. This checking might prove costly, and even it would not always permit the appropriate assignment of rewards and punishments for performance. Employees A, B, and C, as the saying goes, might become very adept at "throwing dead cats in their neighbor's backyard" when substandard performance required accounting for.

A Theory Y job requires but a single external check. Also, responsibility is more easily pinpointed, and the burdens of integration of operations are lessened substantially.

WEB OF FAVORABLE CONSEQUENCES

A web of favorable consequences spins out from the job design of Theory Y, *at any level of the organization.* For low-level jobs, the task is a meaningful whole for employees, boredom is less of a factor, and feedback concerning performance is facilitated. Many of the same features characterize supervisory or managerial jobs organized in line with Theory Y—for example, the supervisor of a work unit performing operations, o_1, o_2, and o_3, versus the supervisor of a work unit performing only one of the operations.

In addition, the Theory Y supervisor gets trained in all phases of operations. His "power" is increased because he controls all operations. The problems of communication and integration are much reduced. And supervisors can reorient their activities around developing those conditions which encourage success rather than punish failure.

As the last point suggests, Theory X and Theory Y imply different styles of supervision. Theory X implies close supervision; that is, the persistent attempt to oversee performance and to give voluminous and detailed instructions. The pressure to integrate the operations of Theory X jobs, of course, encourages this type of supervision. If employee B failed on operation o_2, down-time at o_1 and o_3 could occur. Output could hit zero.

OTHER WORKERS NOT AFFECTED

Theory Y does not operate under the same pressure. If employee B is having a bad time, the trouble spot is obvious and other workers are not affected. Output would fall by a third at a maximum.

Consequently, Theory Y supports general supervision; that is, supervisory concern with developing objectives and measures of performance, the employee being given substantial room for his own tastes and abilities in achieving these objectives. Competition among employees A, B, and C also would encourage a high degree of self-control, as opposed to supervisory control.

The difference between the styles of supervision of the two theories is not niggling. Research shows that general supervision is associated more frequently with high output than is close supervision. Thus of 46 cases in one study, *only* 13 revealed the relation of close supervision with high output or of general supervision with low output. The remaining 33 cases showed that close supervision was associated with low output and general supervision with high output.

That is, backing Theory X and its associated style of supervision paid off in only 28 per cent of the cases. These are the long odds that early workers like Taylor played obsessively. This obsession sometimes paid off handsomely, especially in early applications when virtually any mechanical improvement outweighed the losses detailed here previously. Increasingly, however, Taylorian techniques require a theory which complements their power.

THEORY Y IS A CLEAR WINNER

There is, in sum, substantial evidence that Taylorian techniques should shake-off the guidance of Theory X. The review of the evidence relevant to routinization, social isolation, span of control, and style of supervision is not exhaustive. Even giving away the biggest possible handicap, however, Theory Y is a clear winner.

Our theory must change as our knowledge grows. The present condition, however, is an uneasy alliance between Theory X and conflicting (but unreconciled) findings such as those relevant to job enlargement. This effort may nudge us closer to a more satisfactory theory.

REFERENCES

1. Burleigh B. Gardner and David G. Moore, *Human Relations in Industry* (Irwin, Chicago, 1950), p. 202.

2. Douglas McGregor presents the parent of this analysis in *The Human Side of Enterprise* (McGraw-Hill, New York, 1960), especially pp. 33-57.

3. Chris Argyris, *Personality and Organization* (Harper, New York, 1957), pp. 123-62.

4. Peter F. Drucker, *The Practice of Management* (Harper, New York, 1954), pp. 291-92.

5. Kurt Lewin, "Group Decision and Social Change," in Theodore M. Newcomb and Eugene L. Hartley, editors, *Readings in Social Psychology* (Holt, New York, 1947), p. 343.

6. Robert T. Golembiewski, *The Small Group* (Univ. of Chicago Press, Chicago, 1962).

7. Raymond H. Van Zelst, "Validation of a Sociometric Regrouping Procedure," *Journal of Abnormal and Social Psychology*, Vol. 47 (April, 1952), pp. 299-301.

8. Robert T. Golembiewski, *Behavior and Organization* (Rand McNally, Chicago, 1962).

9. Robert L. Kahn and Daniel Katz, "Leadership Practices in Relation to Productivity and Morale," in *Group Dynamics*, edited by Dorwin Cartwright and Alvin Zander (Row, Peterson, Evanston, Ill., 1953), pp. 617-18 and 619.

10. James C. Worthy, cited in William F. Whyte, *Man and Organization* (Irwin, Homewood, Ill., 1959), pp. 11-16.

11. Jacob I. Hurwitz, Alvin F. Zander, and Bernard Hymovitch, "Some Effects of Power on the Relations Among Group Members," in Cartwright and Zander, *op. cit.*, pp. 483-92.

ADDITIONAL READINGS FOR CHAPTER 1

Argyris, Chris, PERSONALITY AND ORGANIZATION (New York: Harper and Row Publishers, Inc., 1957).

McGregor, Douglas, THE HUMAN SIDE OF ENTERPRISE (New York: McGraw-Hill Book Company, 1960).

——————————, LEADERSHIP AND MOTIVATION (Cambridge, Massachusetts: The M.I.T. Press, 1966).

——————————, THE PROFESSIONAL MANAGER (New York: McGraw-Hill Book Company, 1967).

Chapter 2

MOTIVATION-HYGIENE THEORY
AND JOB ENRICHMENT

McGregor reported in "The Human Side of Enterprise" that managers often ask, "Why aren't people more productive? We pay good wages, provide good working conditions, have excellent fringe benefits. Yet people do not seem to be willing to put forth more than minimum effort." His response to this question was in terms of Maslow's concept of the hierarchy of needs:

> The fact that management has provided for these physiological and safety needs has shifted the motivational emphasis to the social and perhaps to the egoistic needs. Unless there are opportunities *at work* to satisfy these higher-level needs, people will be deprived; and their behavior will reflect this deprivation. Under such conditions, if management continues to focus its efforts on physiological needs, its efforts are bound to be ineffective.

It would seem particularly likely that well-paid, secure managerial and professional employees are relatively well satisfied in their physiological, safety, and social needs. For such people, then, the higher order needs for esteem and status and for self-realization and fulfillment would be operative. The job must satisfy these unmet needs if it is to motivate. The lower order needs, however, cannot be ignored; levels of satisfaction must be maintained or else lower order needs can again be prepotent as active dissatisfactions.

The distinction between those factors that motivate people at work and those that serve only to avoid dissatisfaction forms the basis for the motivation theory and policy implications advanced and illustrated in the following three articles. The first article, by Frederick Herzberg, presents the motivation-hygiene concept, which distinguishes two classes of factors affecting employee attitudes

30

toward work: (1) motivating factors, such as work itself, task achievement, recognition, responsibility, and advancement—factors that are inherent in performing the job itself and that yield satisfaction; and (2) hygiene factors, such as pay, working conditions, company policies, supervision, and interpersonal relations—factors that are extrinsic to performing the job, but that form the environment within which work is done and are sources of dissatisfaction.

In an interesting comparative analysis, Keith Davis links Herzberg's motivating and hygiene factors with Maslow's need hierarchy.[1] Davis suggests that work itself, achievement, recognition, responsibility, and advancement all contribute to meeting needs for self-realization and fulfillment and for esteem and status. On the other hand, pay, working conditions, company policies, supervision, and interpersonal relations contribute to meeting social, safety, and physiological needs. The implications for management are extremely important. Through task specialization, work simplification, and development of standard operating procedures, manangement often builds jobs whose intrinsic features make for both underutilization and underdevelopment of manpower. At the same time, genuinely solicitous of employee well-being, management may conscientiously improve the climate or environment surrounding the work to try to increase employee motivation. The results are disappointing.

Thus, the perplexed manager asks the question McGregor reports: "Why aren't people more productive? We pay good wages, provide good working conditions, have excellent fringe benefits." The manager's question affords a glimpse of his implicit theory of motivation and the policy actions he derives from his theory. His next statement hints that the fault is in the nature of people: ". . . people do not seem willing to put forth more than minimum effort."

If this lack of individual productivity is the same condition that McGregor's Theory X manager witnesses when he assumes that man is inherently lazy, then Herzberg's theory offers new concepts which explain its origins in different terms. Extending the ideas of Chapter 1, Herzberg's analysis leads to conceiving of the same symptoms, laziness and indifference, as human responses to the impact of work impoverished of intrinsic sources of feelings of achievement and responsibility. The manager in our example assumes that his actions to avoid worker dissatisfaction with the conditions surrounding work will produce motivation. How would you expect Herzberg to challenge this assumption?

The work of M. Scott Myers, as summarized in the second article in this chapter, reports research on sources of motivation and hygiene factors for different groups of employees at Texas Instruments, Incorporated. There appear to be significant differences between the job-based sources of motivation for scientists, manufacturing supervisors, and assemblers. What predictions would you be willing to make about differences in motivation and hygiene factors in these jobs?

[1] Keith Davis, *Human Relations at Work*, 3rd ed. (New York: McGraw-Hill Book Company, 1967), p. 37.

The third article, by Robert N. Ford, reports the application of the motivation-hygiene theory at American Telephone and Telegraph. If work itself is the critical and underutilized source of motivators, it follows that motivation may be increased by making jobs richer in stimulating tasks and responsibilities. Ford describes one of numerous instances in which AT&T experimented with job enrichment. The job of keypunch operator was altered so that individual keypunch operators were responsible to particular "customers," that is, other groups inside the company, for completion of a whole task, such as keypunching the payroll for a department.

At the same time, a control group of keypunch operators had no changes made in their jobs. What performance differences would you predict between the control group and the experimental group? What differences in turnover and absenteeism would you predict within the experimental group before and after job enrichment?

A few additional questions may help guide your analysis of the following articles and help you relate them to general management issues. What effect will alternative styles of supervision—say, those based on Theory X and those based on Theory Y—be likely to have, according to Herzberg, in determining the contents of jobs and, consequently, upon employee motivation? How does Herzberg equate or link satisfaction and motivation? Do you concur with his reasoning? What role can the personnel department play in motivation? What do the concepts of the motivation-hygiene theory contribute to your thinking about the management practices McGregor discusses as consistent with Theory Y: decentralization and delegation, job enlargement, and participation and consultative management? Would you expect similar or dissimilar human responses to these practices, given the presence of individual employee personality differences? What weaknesses do you see in job enrichment? Can pay contribute to satisfying needs for status and esteem as well as to satisfying safety and physiological needs?

The Motivation-Hygiene Concept and Problems of Manpower

Frederick Herzberg

I wish to preface my remarks in this article with a disclaimer of competence in the field of manpower. My research and contemplative efforts are more directly related to an equally large and protean problem, that of industrial mental health. From my investigations in the latter area, I have formulated a general theory of mental health, and a specific application to job attitudes that may have bearing on certain aspects of "manpower" questions.

I apologize to the reader who already has familiarity with the Motivation-Hygiene theory of job attitudes for occupying the next few pages with a repetition of data and comments which have appeared a number of times elsewhere. I must lay the groundwork for my thoughts on "manpower" by first presenting my theory of job attitudes, without which I have very little excuse for accepting the invitation to contribute to this issue.

The Motivation-Hygiene theory of job attitudes began with a depth interview study of over 200 engineers and accountants representing Pittsburgh industry. (10) These interviews probed sequences of events in the work lives of the respondents to determine the factors that were involved in their feeling exceptionally happy and conversely exceptionally unhappy with their jobs. From a review and an analysis of previous publications in the general area of job attitudes, a two-factor hypothesis was formulated to guide the original investigation. This hypothesis suggested that the factors involved in producing job satisfaction were separate and distinct from the factors that led to job dissatisfaction. Since separate factors needed to be considered depending on whether job satisfaction or job dissatisfaction was involved, it followed that

Reprinted by permission from the January-February, 1964 issue of *Personnel Administration.* Copyright 1964, Society for Personnel Administration, 485-87 National Press Building, 14th and F Streets, N.W., Washington, D.C. 20004.

these two feelings were not the obverse of each other. The opposite of job satisfaction would not be job dissatisfaction, but rather *no* job satisfaction; and similarly the opposite of job dissatisfaction is *no* job dissatisfaction—not job satisfaction. The statement of the concept is awkward and may appear at first to be a semantic ruse, but there is more than a play with words when it comes to understanding the behavior of people on jobs. The fact that job satisfaction is made up of two unipolar traits is not a unique occurrence. The difficulty of establishing a zero point in psychology with the procedural necessity of using instead a bench mark (mean of a population) from which to start our measurement, has led to the conception that psychological traits are bipolar. Empirical investigations, however, have cast some shadows on the assumptions of bipolarity; one timely example is a study of conformity and nonconformity, where they were shown not to be opposites, but rather two separate unipolar traits.(3)

METHODOLOGY

Before proceeding to the major results of the original study, three comments on methodology are in order. The investigation of attitudes is plagued with many problems, least of which is the measurement phase; although, it is measurement to which psychologists have hitched their scientific integrity. First of all, if I am to assess a person's feeling about something, how do I know he has a feeling? Too often we rely on his say so, even though opinion polling is replete with instances in which respondents gladly respond with all shades of feeling when in reality they have never thought of the issue and are devoid of any practical affect. They respond to respond and we become deceived into believing that they are revealing feelings or attitudes. Secondly, assuming the respondent does have genuine feelings regarding the subject under investigation, are his answers indicative of his feelings; or are they rationalizations, displacements from other factors which are for many reasons less easy to express, coin of the realm expressions for his particular job classification, etc.? Those who have had experience with job morale surveys recognize these ghosts and unfortunately some have contributed to the haunting of companies. Thirdly, how do you equate feelings? If two persons state that they are happy with their jobs, how do you know they are equally happy? We can develop scales, but in truth we are only satisfying our penchant for rulers which do not get inside the experience and measure the phenomenological reality, but rather have significance wholly within our devices.

To meet these objections, the methodology of the original study was formulated. It included a study of changes in job attitudes in the hope that if attitudes change there is more likelihood that an attitude exists. Further, it focused on experiences in the lives of the respondents which contained substantive data that could be analyzed apart from the interpretations of the respondents. Finally, rather than attempt to measure degree of feeling, it focused on peak experiences and contrasted negative peaks with positive peaks; without being concerned with the equality of the peaks. Briefly, we asked our respondents to describe periods in their lives when they were exceedingly happy and unhappy with their jobs. Each respondent gave as many "sequences of events" as he could which met certain criteria including a marked change in feeling, a beginning and an end, and contained some substantive descriptive description other than feelings and interpretations.

A rational analysis of the "sequences of events" led to the results shown in the accompanying chart. For a more complete description of the methodology as well as the results, see *The Motivation to Work*. (10)

The proposed hypothesis appears verified. The factors on the right that led to satisfaction (achievement, recognition for achievement, intrinsic interest in the work, responsibility, and advancement) are mostly unipolar; that is, they contribute very little to job dissatisfaction. Conversely, the dissatisfiers (company policy and administrative practices, supervision, interpersonal relationships, working conditions, and salary) contribute very little to job satisfaction.

SATISFIERS AND DISSATISFIERS

What is the explanation for such results? Do the two sets of factors have two separate themes? It appears so, for the factors on the right all seem to describe man's relationship to what he does, to his job content, achievement on a task, recognition for task achievement, the nature of the task, responsibility for a task, and professional advancement or growth in task capability.

What is the central theme for the dissatisfiers? Restating the factors as the kind of administration and supervision received in doing the job, the nature of interpersonal relationships and working conditions that surround the job, and the amount of salary that accrues to the individual for doing his job, suggests the distinction with the "satisfier" factors. Rather than describing man's relationship to what he does, the "dissatisfier" factors describe his relationship to the context or environment in which he does his job. One cluster of factors relates to what the person does and the other to the situation in which he does it.

As usual with any new theory, a new jargon is invented, perhaps to add some fictitious uniqueness to the theory, although I prefer to think that these new terms better convey the meaning of the theory. Because the factors on the left serve primarily as preventatives, that is to prevent job dissatisfaction, and because they also deal with the environment, I have named these factors "the hygiene" factors in a poor analogy with the way the term is used in preventive medicine. The factors on the right I call the "motivators" because other results indicate they are necessary for improvement in performance beyond that pseudo-improvement which in substance amounts to coming up to a "fair day's work."

In these terms we can recapitulate the major findings of the original study by stating that it is the hygiene factors that affect job dissatisfaction and the motivator factors that affect job satisfaction; with the further understanding that there are two parallel continua of satisfactions. I have only reported on the first study because of the required brevity of this paper. Corroboration can be found in the studies with the following references: (1), (2), (4), (13), (14), (15), (16).

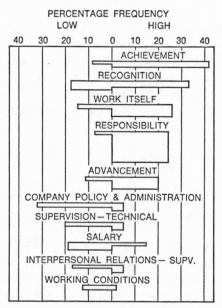

Figure 1. *Comparison of satisfiers and dissatisfiers.*
The wider the box the longer the duration of the attitude.
(Reproduced from The Motivation to Work, *Frederick Herzberg, et al.*
John Wiley and Sons, New York, 1959, by permission of
the publisher.)

SIGNIFICANCE OF HYGIENE FACTORS

Why? We next explore the reasons given by our respondents for the differential effects that the two sets of factors have on job attitudes. In brief, the hygiene factors meet man's needs to avoid unpleasantness. "I don't like to be treated this way; I don't want to suffer the deprivation of low salary; bad interpersonal relationships make me uncomfortable." In other words they want their lives to be hygienically clean. The motivator factors on the other hand make people happy with their jobs because they serve man's basic and human need for psychological growth; a need to become more competent. A fuller commentary on these two separate needs of man are contained in the following publications: (5), (6), (7), (8), (10), (11), (12).

This theory opens wide the door for reinterpretations of industrial relations phenomena. To begin with, job attitudes must be viewed twice; what does the employee seek—what makes him happy; and then a separate question not deducible from the first, what does he wish to avoid—what makes him unhappy? Industrial relations that stress sanitation as their modus operandi can only serve to prevent dissatisfactions and the resultant personnel problems. Of course such attention to hygienic needs is important, for without it any organization, as we well know, will reap the consequences of unhappy personnel. The error of course lies in assuming that prevention will unleash positive health and the returns of increased productivity, lowered absenteeism, turnover, and all the other indices of manpower efficiency. One additional deduction from the theory which is supported by empirical findings should be added. The effect of improved hygiene lasts for only a short time. In fact man's avoidance needs are recurrent and of an infinite variety, and as such we will find that demands for improved salary, working conditions, interpersonal relations and so on will continue to occupy the personnel administrator without any hope of escaping the "what have you done for me lately."

There is nothing wrong with providing the maximum of hygienic benefits to the employee, as much as the society can afford (which appears to be more than the historic cries of anguish which have always accompanied the amelioration of work hygiene would indicate). What is wrong is the summation of human needs in totally hygienic terms. The consequences of this onesided view of man's nature has led to untoward consequences of much greater import than the direct monetary costs of these programs to our organizations. The more pertinent effect has been on the psychological premises of industrial relations and its effect in turn on the self concepts of the employees.

Since hygiene is the apparent key to industrial success, the motivators are given but lip service, and attention to the challenge and meaningfulness of jobs is satisfied via the pious espousal of cultural noises. We are today familiar with the industrial engineering principle of leveling jobs down to the lowest common talent as it applies to the rank and file assembly operation. The same denigration of human talent at the managerial and professional level, the sacrificing of human performance and potentiality to insure that no one will fail or make for unpleasantness, is obscured by referring to the rank and file when acknowledging the lack of meaning in work. At these higher levels, the effects of the assembly line are accomplished by the overuse of rules and regulations, rational organizational principles and the insidious use of interpersonal *skills*. We find that more and more training and education is required to do less and less; more and more effort on surround and less and less substance on accomplishment. Pride in work, in successful accomplishment, in maximizing one's talent is becoming socially gauche or more tragically a victim of progress. We cry for nurturance of human talent and find that we have no place for most of it; human talent on the job has become as much of a surplus commodity as our wheat. And where are our personnel managers? Their problem is hygiene, not the creative function of maximizing human resources.

SIGNIFICANCE OF MOTIVATORS

The Protestant Ethic is being replaced by an Avoidance Ethic in our world of work, and those in charge of personnel utilization have almost totally directed their efforts to maintenance procedures. This is seen from the very beginning of employment in the practice of college recruitment on the campus, where each company sets up its own enticing tent, and selection is transformed into public relations, luring of candidates, and in fact the incredible situation of the candidate interviewing the interviewer.

Job attitude data suggest that after the glow of the initial year on the job, job satisfaction plummets to its lowest level in the work life of individuals. (9) From a life time of diverse learning, successive accomplishment through the various academic stages, and periodic reinforcement of efforts, the entrant to our modern companies finds, that rather than work providing an expanding psychological existence, the opposite occurs; and successive amputations of his self-conceptions, aspirations, learning, and talent are the consequence of earning a living. Of course as the needs and values of our industrial enterprises have become the template for all aspects of our lives, the university is preparing many young people by performing the amputations early, and they enter already primed for work as only a means of hygienic improvement; or for those still capable of enjoying the exercise of their human talents, as means of affording off the job satisfactions. If the number of management development programs is a valid sign, the educational system has done its job too well.

A reaction to retirement policies is beginning to set in as the personal consequences of organizational definitions of human obsolescence are being told. Prior to retirement, however, are 30 to 40 years of partial retirement and partial commitment to work for the too many who have not "succeeded" in terms of organizational advancement. From the first orientation to the farewell party, the history of work careers is a history of human waste. What a paradox we face. There is a shortage of talent in the country at a time when our problems are defined in planetary dimensions and to meet these circumstances we have evolved a system and a philosophy to use and motivate our talent that serves to decrease further this precious resource.

What alternatives are there? A spate of new research and literature is becoming available that is reacting to personnel and managerial psychology that has too long tried to emulate the vast and short term goals of the military. The new literature while encompassing diverse problems, exhortations, solutions and conceptions, seems to have the common theme of emphasizing the motivator needs of man and the necessity for the personnel function of industry to pause in its search for the Holy Grail of instruments, to become creative in finding ways to meet the motivator needs. Man is distinguished from all other animals in that he alone is a determiner. How strange that when it comes to the satisfactions of his special psychological growth needs he finds himself a victim of outside determinisms and helpless in affecting the way he is utilized in work. The short term economic "necessities" cannot justify the larger economic loss and the denial of human satisfaction that the restriction of human talent inevitably costs. I might add that many of the barriers to fuller utilization of manpower that are "justified" by economic reasons are, in reality, devices of fearful and inadequate managers who are not prepared to meet the challenge of managing adults. The philosophy of management which prizes such men is changeable. We need a goal of industry which includes the expansion of manpower utilization in addition to the expansion of productivity and profit. The acceptance of such a goal as basic will lead to the means for its implementation. Personnel cannot remain the one management function that only establishes objectives for which techniques and procedures are available.

REFERENCES

1. Fantz, R. Motivation factors in rehabilitation. *Unpublished doctoral dissertation, Western Reserve University Library*, Cleveland, 1961.

2. Gibson, J. Sources of job satisfaction and job dissatisfaction. *Unpublished doctoral dissertation, Western Reserve University Library*, Cleveland, 1961.

3. Guilford, J. P., Christensen, P. R., Bond, N. and Sutton, M. A factor analysis study of human interests. *Res. Bull.*, 53-11, Human Resources Research Center, San Antonio, 1953.

4. Hamlin, R. and Nemo, R. Self-actualization in choice scores of improved schizophrenics. *J. Clin. Psychol.*, 18, 1962.

5. Herzberg, F. New approaches in management organization and job design. *Industrial Med. and Surgery*, November, 1962.

6. ————, Basic needs and satisfactions of individuals. *Industrial Relations Monograph*, No. 21, Industrial Relations Counselors, Inc., New York, 1962.

7. ————, Comment on the Meaning of Work. Proceedings of symposium of the Worker in the New Industrial Environment. *Industrial Med. and Surgery*, June, 1963.

8. ————, The meaning of work to the individual. In, *Basic Psychology and Physiology of Work*, edited by H. Hellerstein, C. C. Thomas Press, Ft. Lauderdale, In Press.

9. ————, et al. Job attitudes: Research and opinion. Psychological Service of Pittsburgh, 1957.

10. ─────, Mausner, B., and Snyderman, B. *The motivation to work.* John Wiley and Sons, New York, 1959.

11. ─────, and Hamlin, R. A. A motivation-hygiene concept of mental health. *Mental Hygiene,* July, 1961.

12. ─────, and Hamlin, R. Motivation-hygiene concept and psychotheraphy. *Mental Hygiene,* July, 1961.

13. Lodahl, T. Patterns of job attitudes in two assembly technologies. *Graduate School of Business and Public Administration, Cornell University,* Ithaca, New York, 1963.

14. Saleh, S. Attitude change and its effect on the pre-retirement period. *Unpublished doctoral dissertation, Western Reserve University Library,* Cleveland, 1962.

15. Schwarz, P. *Attitudes of middle management personnel.* American Institute for Research, Pittsburgh, 1961.

16. Schwartz, M., Jenusaitis, E. and Stark, H. Motivation factors among supervisors in the utility industry. *Personnel Psychology,* 16, 1963.

Who Are Your Motivated Workers?

M. Scott Myers

What motivates employees to work effectively?

A challenging job which allows a feeling of achievement, responsibility, growth, advancement, enjoyment of work itself, and earned recognition.

What dissatisfies workers?

Mostly factors which are peripheral to the job—work rules, lighting, coffee breaks, titles, seniority rights, wages, fringe benefits, and the like.

When do workers become dissatisfied?

When opportunities for meaningful achievement are eliminated and they become sensitized to their environment and begin to find fault.

These and other interesting conclusions have been drawn from a six-year study of motivation research conducted at Texas Instruments Incorporated. This company's need for answers stemmed from its remarkable growth, for during the 1950's Texas Instruments grew from 1,700 to 17,000 employees, and from annual sales of $2 million to over $200 million. TI's take-off was sparked by a philosophy of management built on informal, shirt-sleeve relationships which fostered informal communication, company identification, and dedicated effort at all levels. Underlying this philosophy was the conviction that *company* goals could be best served by providing opportunities for employees to achieve their *personal* goals.

Highly motivated employees and managers found it easy during the growth years to overlook or take in stride existing and latent problems associated with supervisory ineptness and communication breakdowns. But when company growth decelerated in 1960, motivation ceased to be self-generating and became increasingly dependent on the skill of supervision.

Reprinted from the *Harvard Business Review*, Vol. 42, No. 1 (January-February, 1964), 73-88, by permission of the author and the publisher.

MEASURE FOR MOTIVATION

Starting in 1958, attempts were made to measure symptoms and causes of motivation and dissatisfaction among company workers. Results, unfortunately, were not easily translatable into remedial action. But in 1960, TI management's interest was aroused by some research done by Professor Frederick Herzberg, chairman of the Psychology Department of Western Reserve University. Herzberg's motivation analysis of engineers and accountants in the Pittsburgh area found that the levels of job satisfaction, motivation, and productivity of engineers and accountants were closely related to two sets of factors:

> *Dissatisfiers* are made up, essentially, of such matters as pay, supplemental benefits, company policy and administration, behavior of supervision, working conditions, and several other factors somewhat peripheral to the task. Though traditionally perceived by management as motivators of people, these factors were found to be more potent as dissatisfiers. High motivation does not result from their improvement, but dissatisfaction does result from their deterioration. Negative motivators can be dissatisfiers too, but not so frequently as the factors just given. For example, while *achievement* is a motivator, *failure to achieve* can, of course, be a dissatisfier.
>
> *Motivators,* for the most part, are the factors of achievement, recognition, responsibility, growth, advancement, and other matters associated with the self-actualization of the individual on the job. Job satisfaction and high production were associated with motivators, while disappointments and ineffectiveness were usually associated with dissatisfiers.

Since Herzberg's research presented a possible key to the motivation problem in TI, the company was eager to test whether his theory could be validly applied to its own workers.

Insights from Personnel. In 1961, research began at TI. From a list of employees chosen because of their representativeness, subjects were selected randomly, with the result that they were distributed almost equally over the three salaried job categories of scientist, engineer, and manufacturing supervisor and the two hourly paid classifications of technician and assembler. All 282 subjects were male (except 52 female hourly assemblers); and all were employed in the Dallas divisions.

A competent personnel administrator interviewed each of the subjects, beginning by explaining the general purpose of the project and the nature of the information required. Next, following Herzberg's interview pattern, the interviewer asked:

Think of a time when you felt exceptionally good or exceptionally bad about your job, either your present job or any other job you have had. This can be either the "long-range" or the "short-range" kind of situation, as I have just described it. Tell me what happened.

After an employee's description of a sequence of events that he felt good about ("favorable") was completely explored, he was asked to tell of a different time when he felt the opposite ("unfavorable"); or, if he had first described an unfavorable sequence of events, he was asked about a favorable sequence. Notes were taken during the interview, and questions interjected as necessary to obtain required details.

A total of 715 sequences were obtained from 282 interviewees—an average of 2.5 sequences per individual. Each of the 715 sequences was classified as "favorable" or "unfavorable" and as "long-range" (strong feelings lasting more than two months) or "short-range" (strong feelings lasting less than two months). As many as 54% of the sequences were favorable, while 59% were long-range. Exhibit 1 shows abbreviated examples of favorable and unfavorable

Exhibit 1. *Sample "favorable" and "unfavorable"*
responses to interview questions by incumbents in five job categories

Scientist—*Favorable.* About six months ago I was given an assignment to develop a new product. It meant more responsibility and an opportunity to learn new concepts. I had to study and learn. It was an entirely different job. I always enjoy learning something new. I had been in basic research where it's difficult to see the end results. Now I'm working much harder because I'm more interested. I'm better suited for this type of work.

Scientist—*Unfavorable.* In the fall of 1961 my group would find problems which needed work. We presented them to our supervisor, and he would say, "Don't bother me with details; we are in trouble in this area and need one person for guidance and I am this person." He assigns the problems. He said, "Do what I say whether you think it will work or not." I wouldn't come in Saturday. Made me want to go home and work on my yard. Negative attitude. Killed my initiative because no matter what I came up with my supervisor wouldn't accept it. At first we tried to convince him but finally gave up. Very few gains made in this environment.

Engineer—*Favorable.* In 1959 I was working on a carefully outlined project. I was free to do as I saw fit. There was never a "no, you can't do this." I was doing a worthwhile job and was considered capable of handling the project. The task was almost impossible, but their attitude gave me confidence to tackle a difficult job. My accomplishments were recognized. It helped me gain confidence in how to approach a problem. It helped me to supervise a small number of people to accomplish a goal. I accomplished the project and gained something personally.

Engineer—*Unfavorable.* In December 1961 I was disappointed in my increase. I was extremely well satisfied with the interview and rating. I was dejected and disillusioned, and I still think about it. I stopped working so much at night as a résult of this increase. My supervisor couldn't say much. He tried to get me more money but couldn't get it approved.

Manufacturing Supervisor—*Favorable.* In September 1961 I was asked to take over a job which was thought to be impossible. We didn't think TI could ship what had been promised. I was told half would be acceptable, but we shipped the entire order! They had confidence in me to think I could do the job. I am happier when under pressure.

Manufacturing Supervisor—*Unfavorable.* In the fall of 1958 I disagreed with my supervisor. We were discussing how many of a unit to manufacture, and I told him I thought we shouldn't make too many. He said, "I didn't ask for your opinion . . . we'll do what I want." I was shocked as I didn't realize he had this kind of personality. It put me in bad with my supervisor and I resented it because he didn't consider my opinion important.

Hourly Male Technician—*Favorable.* In June 1961 I was given a bigger responsibility though no change in job grade. I have a better job, more interesting and one that fits in better with my education. I still feel good about it. I'm working harder because it was different from my routine. I am happier . . . feel better about my job.

Hourly Male Technician—*Unfavorable.* In 1962 I was working on a project and thought I had a real good solution. A professional in the group but not on my project tore down my project bit by bit in front of those I worked with. He made disparaging remarks. I was unhappy with the man and unhappy with myself. I thought I had solved it when I hadn't. My boss smoothed it over and made me feel better. I stayed away from the others for a week.

Hourly Female Assembler—*Favorable.* About two weeks ago I wire-welded more transistors than anyone had ever done—2,100 in nine hours. My foreman complimented me, and I still feel good. Meant self-satisfaction and peace of mind to know I'm doing a good job for them. Once you've done it, you want to do it every day, but you can't. It affected my feelings toward everyone. My old foreman came and talked to me. I didn't think I could ever wire-weld.

Hourly Female Assembler—*Unfavorable.* For a while the foreman was partial to one of the girls on the line. She didn't work as hard as the other girls and made phone calls. It got to the point where we went to the man over her foreman and complained. We were all worried since we are afraid of reprisals. . . . The girls don't act the same toward each other now because they are afraid. It affects everyone's work. It has been going on for such a long time it's uncomfortable. It is being stopped now by the foreman's supervisor and that girl has been moved.

---

sequences obtained for each of the five job categories we investigated. Employee responses were further broken down according to job category and sex of respondent. Following this, elements within the sequences were divided into:

> *First-level factors*—the actual events or circumstances leading to favorable or unfavorable feelings.
> *Second-level factors*—the explanations given by respondents as to *why* the event (the first-level factor) caused the favorable or unfavorable feelings.

FIRST-LEVEL FACTORS

Based on collective judgments of the interviewer and project head, 14 first-level factors were identified. Exhibit 2 lists these factors and the number of sequences grouped under each factor. It shows *achievement* to be the largest category, accounting for 33% of the sequences. *Achievement* is comprised of about twice as many favorable responses as unfavorable ones. Conversely, *company policy and administration* (the employee's perception of company organization, goals, policies, procedures, practices, or rules) accounts for more than four times as many unfavorable as favorable responses. Since this exhibit includes data from *all five job categories*, it does not reflect differences among job categories. Consequently, a further category-by-category breakdown is necessary.

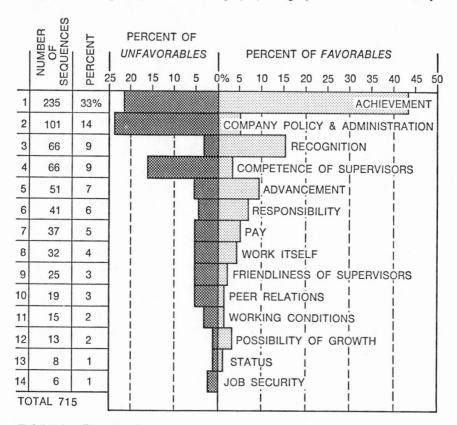

	NUMBER OF SEQUENCES	PERCENT	PERCENT OF UNFAVORABLES	PERCENT OF FAVORABLES
1	235	33%		ACHIEVEMENT
2	101	14		COMPANY POLICY & ADMINISTRATION
3	66	9		RECOGNITION
4	66	9		COMPETENCE OF SUPERVISORS
5	51	7		ADVANCEMENT
6	41	6		RESPONSIBILITY
7	37	5		PAY
8	32	4		WORK ITSELF
9	25	3		FRIENDLINESS OF SUPERVISORS
10	19	3		PEER RELATIONS
11	15	2		WORKING CONDITIONS
12	13	2		POSSIBILITY OF GROWTH
13	8	1		STATUS
14	6	1		JOB SECURITY
TOTAL 715				

Exhibit 2 *First-level factors.*

Personality Differences. But before the results of this analysis are presented, it is necessary that we point out that the potency of any of the job factors mentioned, as a motivator or dissatisfier, is not solely a function of the nature of the factor itself. It is also related to the personality of the individual.

For most individuals, the greatest satisfaction and the strongest motivation are derived from *achievement, responsibility, growth, advancement, work itself,* and *earned recognition.* People like this, whom Herzberg terms "motivation seekers," are motivated primarily by the nature of the task and have high tolerance for poor environmental factors.

"Maintenance seekers," on the other hand, are motivated primarily by the nature of their environment and tend to avoid motivation opportunities. They are chronically preoccupied and dissatisfied with maintenance factors surrounding the job, such as pay, supplemental benefits, supervision, working conditions, status, job security, company policy and administration, and fellow employees. Maintenance seekers realize little satisfaction from accomplishment and express cynicism regarding the positive virtues of work and life in general. By contrast, motivation seekers realize great satisfaction from accomplishment and have positive feelings toward work and life in general.

Maintenance seekers show little interest in kind and quality of work, may succeed on the job through sheer talent, but seldom profit professionally from experience. Motivation seekers enjoy work, strive for quality, tend to overachieve, and benefit professionally from experience.

Maintenance seekers are usually outer-directed and may be highly reactive or ultraconservative. Their values tend to blow with the wind and take on the coloring of the environment (such as parroting top management, or acting more like top management than top management itself). Motivation seekers are more often inner-directed, self-sufficient persons whose belief systems are deliberately chosen and developed, and are less subject to influence by the environment.

Although an individual's orientation as a motivation seeker or a maintenance seeker is fairly permanent, it can be influenced by the characteristics of his various roles. For example, maintenance seekers in an environment of achievement, responsibility, growth, and earned recognition tend to behave like and acquire the values of motivation seekers. On the other hand, the absence of motivators causes many motivation seekers to behave like maintenance seekers, and to become preoccupied with the maintenance factors in their environment.

All of the five occupational groups discussed below, except female assemblers, seem to be largely comprised of actual or potential motivation seekers. Scientists are the group most strongly oriented as motivation seekers, and female assemblers those most strongly oriented as maintenance seekers. Maintenance seeking among female assemblers probably stems from the tradition of circumscribed and dependent roles of women in industry as well as from their supervisors' failure to provide them with motivation opportunities.

Now let us examine each occupational group in detail.

Scientist.   Exhibit 3 shows the distribution of first-level factors for scientists. The length of the color bars on the upper side of the transparent horizontal plane indicates the percentage of favorable sequences or events classified under each factor. For example, 50% of the favorable sequences relate to achievement. The other 50% are distributed among the other six categories shown in color on the upper side. Similarly, black bars on the lower side show the frequency distribution of "unfavorable" sequences. Factors whose combined "favorables" and "unfavorables" represented less than 5% of the sequences for a given job category have not been charted for that category.

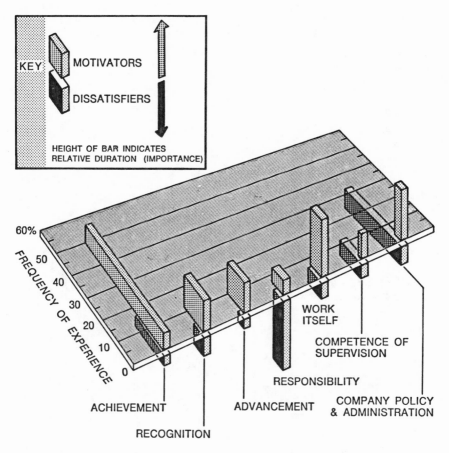

Exhibit 3.   *Factors affecting motivation of scientists.*

Earlier the terms "motivators" and "dissatisfiers" were defined. In Exhibit 3, those factors which extend predominantly above the plane are clearly "motivators," for these are not peripheral to the job itself. In fact, the motivators listed in this and the following charts relate to motivation needs which are *closely* associated with job performance. Bars extending predominantly below are "dissatisfiers," or maintenance factors, since their satisfaction serves to avoid dissatisfaction rather than to stimulate motivation, and since they are peripheral to the task.

The height of the bars in Exhibit 3 shows duration of feelings, based on the ratio of number of long-lasting to short-term feelings. The duration of feelings, in turn, reflects their relative importance to the individual. Note, in the case of scientists, that long-lasting good feelings are often associated with *work itself* and that long-lasting bad feelings stem from *responsibility* disappointments.

Engineers. These employees reveal a pattern similar to that shown by scientists. Exhibit 4.A contains all factors found on the scientists' chart, plus *friend-*

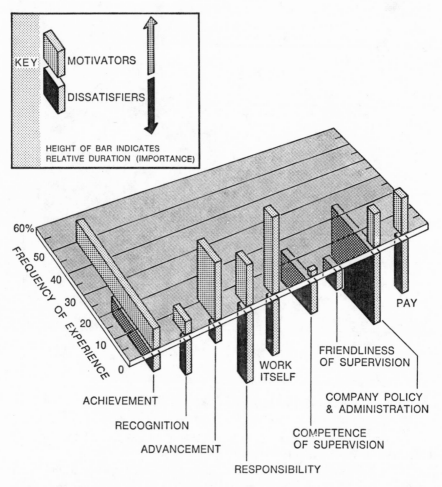

Exhibit 4.A *Factors affecting motivation of engineers.*

liness of supervision and *pay*. This is not to imply that these two factors are not important to the scientists, but rather that they do not rate as high a priority in the scientists' hierarchy of needs.

Manufacturing Supervisors.   In Exhibit 4.B we see a pattern which differs significantly from that of the scientists or engineers. The tallness of the *advancement, growth,* and *responsibility* bars reflects a higher aspiration toward success through administration than was apparent for scientists and engineers. Note that *work itself* is not even mentioned by manufacturing supervisors, but *possibility of growth* and *peer relations* appear as new factors.

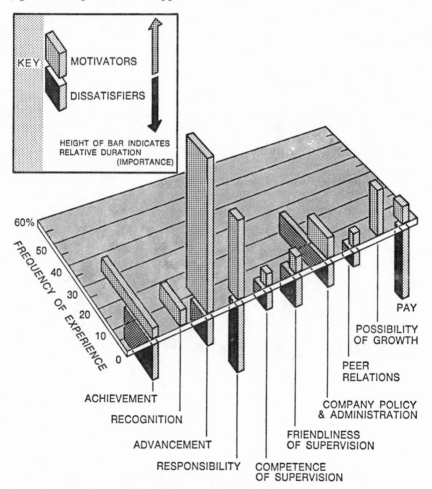

Exhibit 4.B.   *Factors affecting motivation of manufacturing supervisors.*

Sequences cited by manufacturing supervisors frequently reflect climbing aspirations. For example, *achievement* is usually more important as a stepping stone to success, and *failure* as a threat to advancement. *Company policy* and *administration* as a maintenance factor functions as a block to advancement, and as a motivation factor it is seen as providing opportunity for achieving career objectives. *Peer relations* as a dissatisfier usually stems from the thwarting of career goals by associates. *Pay,* for the manager, usually signifies success or failure and, in terms of duration of feelings, is more potent as a dissatisfier than as a motivator.

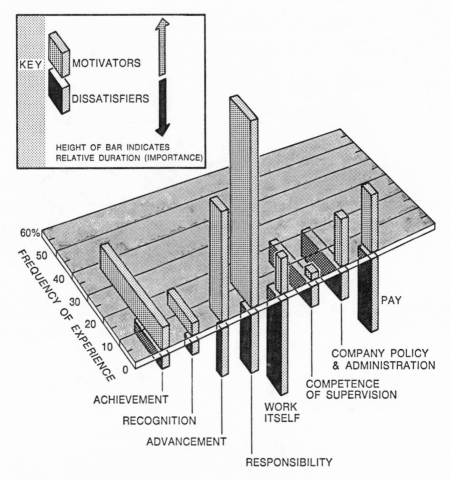

Exhibit 4.C.   *Factors affecting motivation of hourly
                    male technicians.*

Hourly Technicians. The pattern of motivators and dissatisfiers in Exhibit 4.C dramatically illustrates the needs of the semiprofessional hourly male technician. The extreme height of the responsibility and advancement bars shows the importance of these factors as motivators to him. Since most hourly paid technicians feel that they have little opportunity to advance and experience a sense of responsibility, the impact of these factors as motivators when they do occur is substantial.

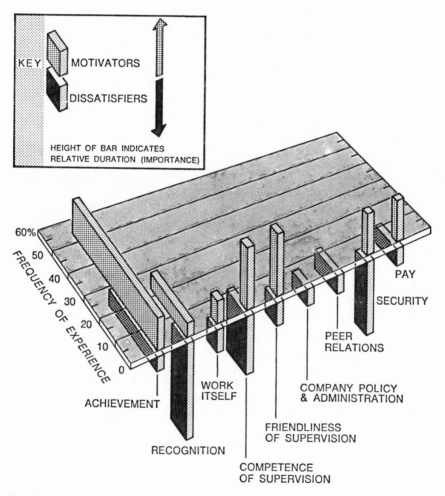

Exhibit 4.D. *Factors affecting motivation of female assemblers.*

The hourly man, usually not a college graduate, tends to see himself in a supportive role, doing the unpleasant and uninteresting tasks which professionals choose to avoid. The importance of *work itself* as a dissatisfier reflects the hourly man's contention that he gets stuck with the dirty work. The *competence of supervision* factor (which refers to the supervisor's skill in planning and organizing work, to his delegating practices, and to his impartiality) emerges as a potent dissatisfier. Similarly, the technician perceives *company policy and administration* as inadequate or unfair in providing opportunities for job satisfaction. *Pay* is an important factor, slightly more so as a dissatisfier than as a motivator. Its greater importance to the hourly male probably stems from the fact that he lives closer to the subsistence level than do salaried persons.

The technician chart (Exhibit 4.C) appears to reflect greater frustrations and hence greater challenge to supervision than do the charts for scientists, engineers, and manufacturing supervisors. Male technicians work at a level of responsibility where supervision is traditionally close. Being males with career aspirations and normal needs for independence (reinforced by TI's philosophy of equality), it is understandable that they sometimes perceive supervision as oppressively restrictive. Perhaps in no other group does the supervisor's success depend to such a degree on his ability to supervise without appearing to do so.

Female Assemblers.   Motivators and dissatisfiers for the female assembler, as Exhibit 4.D shows, reflect motivational needs significantly different from those of other job categories. However, not all of the differences are evident from the chart. For example, *achievement*, the most potent motivator for all classifications, derives its primary importance for the female from the affirmation it wins from her supervisor. Note that the *recognition* bars show favorable recognition to be an important short-range motivator, and unfavorable recognition or the lack of recognition as a long-lasting dissatisfier.

It is interesting to note that *work itself*, generally thought to be oppressively routine, is mentioned as often as a motivator as it is as a dissatisfier. *Pay* for the female assembler emerges about five times more often as a dissatisfier than as a motivator. Though *peer relations* does not appear in this exhibit as a motivator, its importance to women is evidenced by its emergence as a dissatisfier when friendly relationships break down. The height of the *competence of supervision* and the *friendliness of supervision* bars indicates the importance of fair, competent, and friendly supervision as satisfiers, and the impact of favoritism, incompetence, and unfriendliness as dissatisfiers. The height of the *security* bar as a dissatisfier probably reflects the lingering impact of layoffs which actually affected only a small number.

The total pattern of the hourly female chart indicates that, unlike the hourly male, she has not found advancement and increased responsibility potent motivators, and she tends to prefer close supervision. Her supervisor should be impartial, competent, decisive, and friendly. Despite women's cherished status of equality, most female assemblers seem to prefer to relate themselves to their supervisor in a dependent role. To these female assemblers, many of whom are single, widowed, or divorced, the supervisor is an important person (sometimes the only one) to whom she can turn for understanding, affirmation, and recognition.

SECOND-LEVEL FACTORS

The factors just analyzed were those revealed by the respondent's description of the actual events leading to his favorable or unfavorable feelings. But this tells only part of the story. As noted, during the information-gathering interview, after the respondent had described a sequence, he was asked what the event *meant* to him, and *why* it made him feel good or bad. The reasons he gave were recorded as second-level factors.

Each sequence usually resulted in two or more such second-level factors one of which was often the same as a first-level factor. Thus, in 70% of those sequences where *achievement* was the first-level factor, it was also named as a second-level factor. Other second-level factors commonly resulting from achievement were *recognition, work itself, pride,* and *growth.* For instance:

> The female assembler, mentioned in Exhibit 1, who wire-welded 2,100 transistors illustrates the classification process. Her first-level factor was "achievement," and her seond-level factors were "recognition," "achievement," and "pride." Achievement was first-level because, as she put it, "I didn't think I could ever wire-weld." But she did! She welded more than anyone had ever done before. However, the *importance* of the event for her stemmed from the second-level factors which she later identified as recognition, a feeling of achievement, and pride.

Exhibit 5 presents the distribution of the 1,255 responses of second-level factors resulting from the 715 sequences charted in Exhibit 2; 9 of the 12 second-level factors also appeared as first-level factors. In Exhibits 5 through 12.B, combined data from all five job categories are given to shed light on the second-level factors which were identified for each of the 14 first-level factors. The pie charts indicate why a given factor is a motivator or dissatisfier (by showing the distribution of second-level factors for the first-level experience). The page-wide horizontal charts portray the first-level factors which contributed to a particular second-level feeling.

Achievement and Failure.   Exhibit 6.A reveals that *achievement* is its own best reward; this is evidenced by the fact that "achievement itself" constitutes 43% of the reasons given as to why an achievement was gratifying.

Exhibit 6.B indicates that *failure* (with 50%) is a dissatisfier for essentially the same reasons that achievement is a motivator. Only *unfairness* and *security* emerge as new factors.

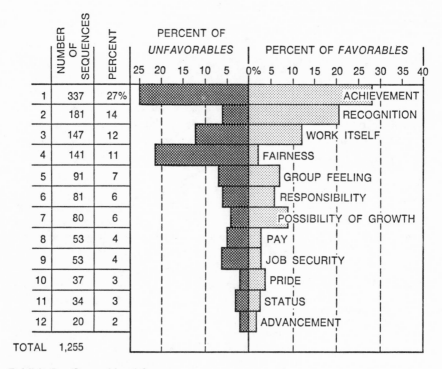

NUMBER OF SEQUENCES	PERCENT	PERCENT OF UNFAVORABLES / PERCENT OF FAVORABLES	
1	337	27%	ACHIEVEMENT
2	181	14	RECOGNITION
3	147	12	WORK ITSELF
4	141	11	FAIRNESS
5	91	7	GROUP FEELING
6	81	6	RESPONSIBILITY
7	80	6	POSSIBILITY OF GROWTH
8	53	4	PAY
9	53	4	JOB SECURITY
10	37	3	PRIDE
11	34	3	STATUS
12	20	2	ADVANCEMENT
TOTAL	1,255		

Exhibit 5.   *Second-level factors.*

Exhibit 7.A, which portrays the first-level factors which caused the second-level feelings of achievement, bears out the adage that "nothing succeeds like success," since feelings of successful achievement stem from a successful achievement in 63% of the cases. The potency of other, seemingly unrelated experiences in causing feelings of achievement in workers is largely a function of individual needs. For example, the realization of a specific personal goal may be felt to be an achievement only by the person affected.

Unlike feelings of achievement, which stem from an act of the doer in about two-thirds of the first-level achievement sequences, feelings of failure usually arise from external forces. As Exhibit 7.B shows, in only 32% of the cases do feelings of failure originate from workers' acknowledged personal failures on the job.

Recognition.   Both motivation and maintenance needs are served by *recognition*. Earned recognition is a manifestation of justice, an act of approval which confirms successful achievement and individual worth. Pay increases and bonuses stemming from merit are tangible acts of recognition. And these are usually potent as motivators for motivation seekers and as dissatisfiers for maintenance seekers.

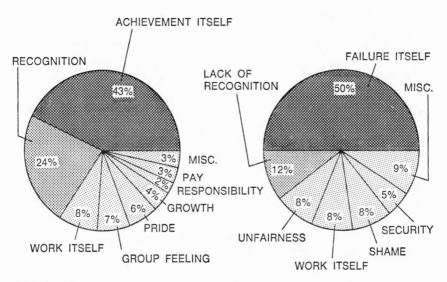

Exhibit 6.A.
Why achievement is a motivator.

Exhibit 6.B.
Why failure is a dissatisfier.

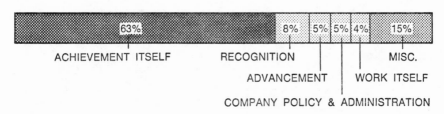

Exhibit 7.A.   *Factors contributing to feelings of achievement.*

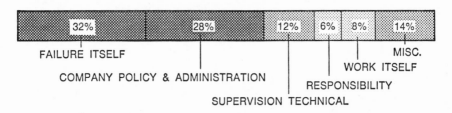

Exhibit 7.B.   *Factors contributing to feelings of failure.*

Unearned recognition, in the form of friendliness, reassurance, small talk, and personal interest, serves to satisfy security, status, and social needs. This type of recognition is not a substitute for earned recognition, but it is essential as a maintenance factor, particularly in the absence of opportunity to earn recognition through job performance.

But recognition as a sustaining force has little lasting value, as evidenced by the shortness of the *security* bars in Exhibits 3 through 4.D. Its potency as a motivator, in view of its short duration, indicates a need for frequent reinforcement. On the other hand, recognition for scientists (Exhibit 3) frequently arises from professional activities and tends to be somewhat longer lasting. The need for meaningful interim recognition for scientists on long-range projects is obvious, and professional activities often serve this need.

Exhibit 8.A shows recognition to be a prime catalyst for other motivational experiences, with recognition itself the most commonly mentioned second-level factor. Perhaps recognition as an end product derives much of its value from the fact that for many workers who personally see only a miniscule portion of the total task, recognition is the only criterion of achievement and progress available to them.

Exhibit 8.B shows the consequences of unfavorable recognition or the failure to receive expected recognition. Recognition disappointments results in dissatisfactions associated with unfairness, work itself, recognition itself, failure,

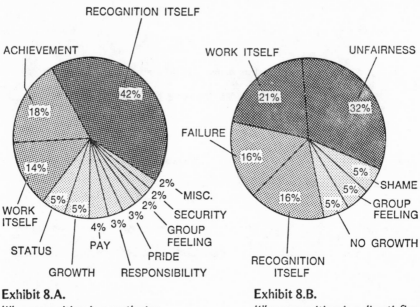

Exhibit 8.A.
Why recognition is a motivator.

Exhibit 8.B.
Why recognition is a dissatisfier.

stymied growth, hostility toward the work group, and shame. The double-edged potential of recognition reflected in these two charts offers no support to the philosophy expressed in the cliché, "If they don't hear from me, they know they're doing O.K."

Pay Itself. The role of pay as an incentive is controversial. Exhibits 3 through 4.D show pay itself not to be particularly influential as either a motivator or dissatisfier. Exhibits 9.A and 9.B indicate that pay derives its importance primarily from the factors it represents. In Exhibit 9.A *pay itself* accounts for only 11% of the reasons for satisfaction and is only one-fourth as important as the recognition it represents. Exhibit 9.B indicates that a disappointment in pay has more impact as an act of unfairness than it has as a loss of pay itself. From comparison of the relative percentages of pay itself on the two charts it appears that pay itself is less potent as a motivator than as a dissatisfier.

Work Itself. Attitudes toward *work itself* are related less to the nature of the task than they are to other factors in the work situation. Exhibit 10.A indicates that a good feeling toward work itself stems from the nature of the task in only 8% of the cases. However, work itself plus all other motivators on the chart accounts for 80% of the good feelings associated with work itself. By contrast, Exhibit 10.B indicates that disenchantment with work itself results more often from maintenance factors.

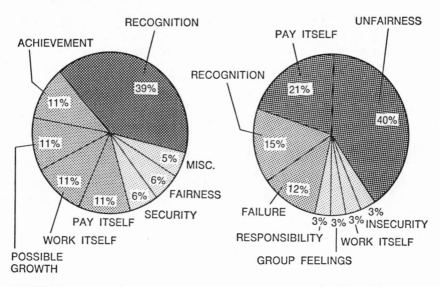

Exhibit 9.A.
Why pay is a motivator.

Exhibit 9.B.
Why pay is a dissatisfier.

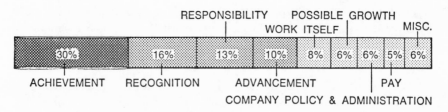

Exhibit 10.A.   *Factors contributing to satisfaction
with work itself.*

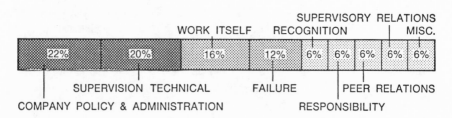

Exhibit 10.B.   *Factors contributing to dissatisfaction
with work itself.*

Fairness.   Positive *fairness* is a negligible second-level factor. On the other hand, *unfairness* is designated by female assemblers more often than any other second-level factor as the reason for unhappiness on the job. Male respondents designate unfairness second only to failure as the explanation of feelings of unhappiness.

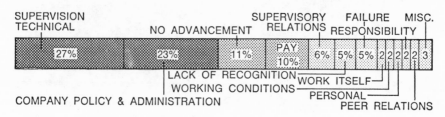

Exhibit 11.   *Factors contributing to feelings of
unfairness.*

Exhibit 11 reveals that feelings of unfairness are most commonly associated with three times as many maintenance factors as are motivation factors.

Supervision.   Although supervisory competence and supervisory relations are discussed as two discrete first-level factors, they are inextricably related to all other first- and second-level factors. Supervisory competence, for example, manifested as delegation, planning and organizing work, and impartiality, has a bearing on the potency of motivators and dissatisfiers in the job environment as evidenced by Exhibits 12.A and 12.B. The first of these exhibits indicates that good feelings about supervision are translated into motivators in three-fourths of the cases, most potent of which are recognition and achievement. Poor supervision as a first-level factor, as Exhibit 12.B shows, results in unhappiness associated with dissatisfiers in more than half the cases.

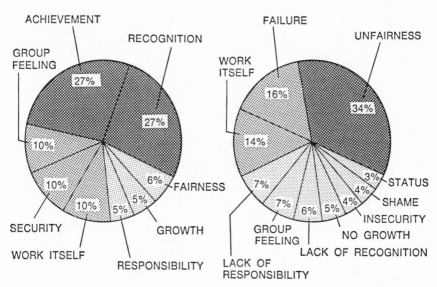

Exhibit 12.A.
*Why good supervision
is a motivator.*

Exhibit 12.B.
*Why poor supervision is
a dissatisfier.*

WELLSPRINGS OF MOTIVATION

This study clearly points out that the factors in the work situation which motivate employees are different from the factors that dissatisfy employees. Motivation stems from the challenge of the job through such factors as achievement, responsibility, growth, advancement, work itself, and earned recognition. Dissatisfactions more often spring from factors peripheral to the task.

Effective job performance depends on the fulfillment of both motivation and maintenance needs. Motivation needs, as Exhibit 13 illustrates, include responsibility, achievement, recognition, and growth, and are satisfied through the media grouped in the inner circle of the exhibit. Motivation factors focus on the individual and his achievement of company and personal goals.

Maintenance needs are satisfied through media listed in the outer circle under the headings of physical, social, status, orientation, security, and economic. Peripheral-to-the-task and usually group-administered maintenance factors have little motivational value, but their fulfillment is essential to the avoidance of dissatisfaction. An environment rich in opportunities for satisfying motivation needs leads to motivation-seeking habits, and a job situation sparse in motivation opportunities encourages preoccupation with maintenance factors.

In other words, in a situation of satisfied motivation needs, maintenance factors have relatively little influence either as satisfiers or dissatisfiers. However, the removal of opportunity for meaningful achievement sensitizes the individual to his environment, and his perception of maintenance factors becomes colored by a readiness to find fault.

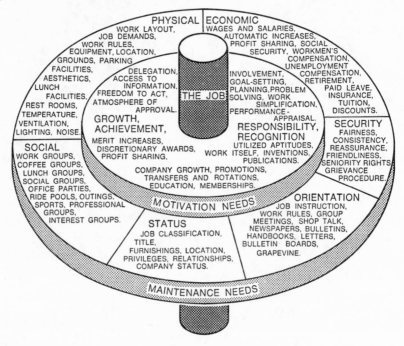

Exhibit 13. *Employee needs—maintenance and motivational.*

Thus motivation, or the achievement of personal goals, is not facilitated by management actions which overrate maintenance needs, but rather by actions which provide conditions of motivation.

The spiraling cost of fringe benefits in business and industry cries out that management is continually making misguided and futile attempts to motivate through maintenance factors. Competition among companies to outdo each other in the realm of maintenance factors, justifiable as it may seem as a competitive measure, fails to increase productivity and probably contributes to the pricing of American products and services out of the world market.

Paradoxically, satisfying motivation needs is not only the more realistic approach for satisfying personal goals and sustaining the organization, but it is also less expensive. The requirements for satisfying motivation needs are competent supervision or perpetual organizational growth. And growth without competent supervision, except in the case of temporary advantage from technological breakthrough or monopoly, is an unrealistic expectation.

The Supervisor's Role.   Simply stated, the supervisor's role is two-fold. He must:

1. Provide conditions of motivation.
2. Satisfy maintenance needs.

Conditions of motivation are task-centered; they depend on supervisors' skill in planning and organizing work. Ideally, the planning and organization of work begin at the top, to provide members at each succeeding organizational level with responsibilities, which in turn can be subdivided into meaningful chunks that challenge capabilities and satisfy aspirations. Matching jobs with people requires a knowledge and control of the task, as well as an understanding of individual aptitudes and aspirations.

Satisfaction of the motivation needs in Exhibit 13 is typically achieved through the mechanisms and media listed in the inner band. In terms of day-to-day behavior patterns, the role of the competent supervisor includes providing each individual with the requisite job information, maintaining high performance expectations, encouraging goal-setting and the exercise of independent judgment, providing recognition and rewards commensurate with achievements, and maintaining an atmosphere of approval in which failure is a basis for growth rather than recrimination.

The maintenance needs listed in Exhibit 13 as economic, security, orientation, status, social, and physical, have many conditions and media for satisfying these needs listed beneath them. The supervisor's support in satisfying these needs is essential, particularly so for security and orientation needs. Feelings of security are largely influenced by the supervisor and determine whether the individual will assert himself in a constructive motivation-seeking manner, or will fall back on maintenance-seeking behavior. The satisfaction of orientation needs requires supervisors steeped in company lore, policies, procedures, and practices. The ability and willingness of supervisors to dispense information when requested meets a need seldom satisfied by handbooks and other written communications. Further, this information-dispensing role of the supervisor, served with friendly small talk, keeps communication channels open.

A PRACTICAL APPLICATION

Rapidly changing industry no longer affords time for the young supervisor to develop competence through an extended trial-and-error apprenticeship. Furthermore, in view of today's increasing technological orientation to business, he is often selected because of his professional competence with hardware. This only increases his need for a simple and practical theory of management that will accelerate his acquisition of managerial know-how.

The concept of maintenance and motivation needs developed here is not strange or abstract but is clearly part of the experience and repertoire of most supervisors, including the straw-boss supervisor of unskilled workers. Moreover, it is easily translatable to supervisory action at all levels of responsibility. It is a framework on which supervisors can evaluate and put into perspective the constant barrage of "helpful hints" to which they are subjected, and hence serves to increase their feelings of competence, self-confidence, and autonomy.

Naturally, to become fully effective, motivation-maintenance theory must find expression in the day-to-day behavior and decisions of supervisors. For those supervisors whose personal adjustment and intuitive judgment endow them with natural aptitude for effective supervision, motivation-maintenance theory offers additional insights and guidance for reinforcing and further developing leadership skills. For them, motivation-maintenance theory finds almost immediate expression. For others, adopting and practicing this approach require an evolutionary process whereby (1) awareness, (2) understanding, (3) conviction, and (4) habit are developed over a period of perhaps five years.

Several mechanisms have been developed in TI to introduce this understanding to supervisors, to reinforce its application, and to audit its effectiveness.

TI's corporate ten-year plan for personnel administration (which is updated annually to support the ten-year operating goals of the corporation) was restructured in 1963 to fit motivation-maintenance theory concepts. Functions performed by personnel were analyzed in terms of their potential for serving maintenance or motivation needs. Next, both the theory and the research on which it was based were thoroughly explained to managers and supervisors at all levels through the medium of large group meetings. Here also these men were informed of the company's plan to implement the theory, and their cooperation was elicited.

Since satisfying employee maintenance needs requires that a company pay attention to the environmental factors shown on the outer circle of Exhibit 13, TI closely examined how effectively newspapers, handbooks, group meetings, wages and salaries, safety and health services, social and recreational programs, and the like were meeting workers' needs.

In order to facilitate the meeting of motivation needs, a training program for supervisors, entitled Seminar in Motivation, was presented to all levels of supervision. Meeting in groups of from six to ten men, supervisors assimilated the theory and gained skills in its application to problems related to their own supervisory responsibility in a series of six two-hour sessions. The intense personal involvement of supervisors in the meetings and initial feedback from their subordinates indicate that these working sessions will meet long-felt needs and result in more effective supervision.

Attitude Survey. Quality of supervision is reflected in job performance, attendance, morale, and ultimately in profits. However, these factors seldom lend themselves to timely or accurate measurement. Since employee attitudes are measurable predictors of behavior, a formalized attitude measurement program structured around the motivation-maintenance frame of reference has been instituted in TI. By this means, total company effectiveness in each of the six maintenance- and the four motivation-need areas can be appraised. A deficiency in one of these need areas, such as security or orientation, signals a need for reinforcing efforts in that area. Administered annually to 10% samples of each of the sixty-odd departments, the attitude survey yields trend data as well as interdepartmental comparisons, and is both a meaningful barometer of supervisory effectiveness and a key to corrective action.

Application and reinforcement of motivation-maintenance theory are also achieved through many other specific media such as performance appraisal, educational assistance, supervisors' newsletters, planning conferences, work simplification, wage and salary administration, statements of policy and procedure, and the maintenance of a system of democratic and informal relationships.

In the final analysis, the workability of a theory of management depends on its integration into the total management process. Further, motivation-maintenance theory, like any theory of managment, is at the mercy of its practitioners and will remain intact and find effective utilization only to the extent that it serves as a mechanism for harnessing constructive motives.

It can be useful as a practical framework for codifying intuitive effectiveness and for guiding the inexperienced, but it will not correct a management failure which, for example, permits the appointment of immature or unscrupulous supervisors. The managment philosophy which sparked the growth of TI created a fertile environment for introducing motivation—maintenance theory as a mechanism for achieving company goals by providing opportunities for employees to achieve personal goals.

"The Obstinate Employee"

Robert N. Ford

I trust that my friend, Professor Raymond A. Bauer, will share with me not only the catchy title of his paper on "The Obstinate Audience,"[1] but that he will also let me draw some parallels between his analysis of the audience situation in general and that of a very special audience, the employee. It would appear that the employee as audience, as someone with whom management is trying to communicate, is becoming more obstinate than ever. We have communicated like mad at him. I'm afraid that he finished listening long before we stopped talking.

TURNOVER AS INDICATOR

The mute testimony to this state of affairs is the ever increasing rate at which employees resign or are dismissed. This problem is being faced by many businessmen, as well as by such other diverse employers as government, hospitals, and the public schools. The total turnover figure, which includes death, retirement, entrance into the armed forces, etc. is not as useful for our analysis as are the resignation-dismissal components.

If I told you that turnover in selected jobs in some locations in some companies runs beyond 100 per cent annually, you had better believe me. Some may say, "That's an impossible rate." No. All you have to do is fill each job more than once per year on the average, and there you are. As you may

Reprinted from *Public Opinion Quarterly,* Vol. 33, No. 3 (Fall, 1969), pp. 301-310, by permission of the author and *Psychology Today* Magazine. Copyright © Communications/ Research/Machines, Inc., Del Mar, California. This article was delivered as the Presidential Address at the Annual Meeting of the American Association for Public Opinion Research, Lake George, New York, May 18, 1969.

guess, selected areas of some large citites are especially troublesome for managers. But I shall lay aside this special environmental situation tonight and talk about the general case of employee disenchantment with work. And I shall not tie the case merely to high turnover. As a friend in Bell Canada remarked, "The turnover is bad enough, Bob, but what really bothers me is that we have lost so many people who are still with us!" Older employees, especially, may feel "locked in," unable to leave. A family situation, for example, can effectively lock a man to his job. Job alienation then shows up in such other ways as reduced productivity, union grievances, absence, tardiness, and a bad grapevine from plant to employment market.

My topic may seem a bit off-beat for an AAPOR audience, but I trust it will appeal to anyone who has employees reporting to him. If turnover is not yet a problem, give thanks for a bit of lead time. Next, I shall predict that this problem, dissatisfaction with work, will become increasingly a public issue, that people in " dum-dum" jobs will become increasingly hard to manage.

THE SOCIAL MODEL

Employees were not precious, really, during the Great Depression. As late as 1940, the president of a university where I taught is said to have remarked about another faculty member, "Let him leave if he wants to. Tell him we'll go down to the nearest filling station and hire another Ph.D." A communication model aimed at changing the level of employee loyalty did not emerge, for there was no felt need to communicate.

During the years of World War II, the power of various one-way communication media was brought to bear by industry in an effort to keep its employees, to get them to produce more or better: movies, company newspapers, magazines, campaigns, prizes, talks to assembled groups or over closed-circuit loudspeakers. More recently, closed circuit television has been added. By 1969, I believe that only a profound optimist would attempt to find any effect of such approaches on turnover or on other manifestations of job dissatisfaction. So I agree with Bauer that the employee audience, like his general audience, can be most obstinate. About what? That is the question; let us move closer to the problem.

TRANSACTIONAL MODEL:
MANAGEMENT AND EMPLOYEE

Those of us lucky enough to have been with Sam Stouffer and Carl Hovland in the War Department during World War II may have first met the transactional model there. What did the soldier think on many issues affecting his very life, his survival? Through the interview and the questionnaire, teams spread around the world did their best to find out. They made these studies for the film makers, for those getting out publications for officers, for any command organization that showed any interest. A publication called "What the Soldier Thinks" was issued monthly for wide distribution to line officers. How effective? Who will ever know. But we were quite sure that this audience, the soldier, *would not hear us, if we would not hear him.*

This model moved into industry rather quickly. The analogy was perfect. The soldier was merely an employee suffereing from a handicap: he could not quit his job. The Bell System hired me in 1947 to work on their employee problems, in the belief that I could bring with me such advanced tools as non-directive and semistructured interviewing, scale analysis, and probability sampling.

Twenty years and one minute later, I want to give you my impression of why not much happened, not until very recently. We were working on the wrong transaction, I now believe. Implicit in the interviewing studies, in the question-naires that were used on a trend basis with thousands and thousands of employees, was the belief that an improved flow of communication from employee to management would provide the basis for a strikingly improved counter-flow. Out of this would emerge better human relations, better attitudes because of mutual understanding about the work to be done, and thence to better service to customers.

We gave up the trend analysis of employee attitudes in the mid-1950's. There were trend lines on such Guttman blocks of questions as attitude toward super-vision, toward the company, toward adequacy of communications, toward the way the company measured productivity; on financial attitudes, financial knowl-edge, and many others. The lines would wobble from year to year, and an organization that had been in 14th place might find itself in 19th or 11th. Those who improved in the rank order became complacent, and the remainder felt that they were not being helped very much. The trend survey of employee attitude quietly disappeared. This transactional model was dead after having been given a first-class trial.

TRANSACTIONAL MODEL: EMPLOYEE AND CUSTOMER

In retrospect, I feel the problem might be parodied thus. A committee of men, all with the best of intentions, all skilled in communications and the arts of presentation, will not come up with a design for an atomic bomb, if that is their problem, unless one of them has enormous knowledge and understanding about physics. Communications are not enough. This was the fix we were in; we needed information.

Professor Frederick Herzberg's book, *The Motivation to Work*,[2] precipitated a drastic change in my thinking. Virtually all the factors on which we had assembled data in the employee attitude surveys would be labeled "hygiene," or maintenance factors, in his theory of work. Herzberg holds that an employee is never happy, or satisfied, or motivated deeply to work by such matters as management policies and administration, supervision, benefit plans, salary plans, or good human relations. He will be unhappy if there are *not* good; they are potential dissatisfiers. He *expects* these external motivators to be good in modern American society. And just as good manners have not stopped our cities from burning, neither have good manners kept employees at work they do not want to perform.

Now, perhaps, we were getting closer to the truth. The work itself was the culprit. The transaction that was not adequately understood was the one between employee and customer, not between employee and management. This—to me—was a bold thought. Forget about money, benefits, human relations; let someone else take care of these since some one *must* do it. Dig in exclusively on the nature of the task assigned to each person. See if it can be improved. Is the task really a constant? Certainly we have treated a job as though a job is a job is a job.

I suppose that there are some tasks in every large organization that are so thin, so lacking in stimulating possibilities that they cannot be enriched. Almost without exception, however, the jobs we worked on could be improved for the incumbents. And I came to believe, as our experimental studies progressed from 1965 to date, that the *natural history of a job is to get worse.* Just as tuberculosis leads to death unless someone with knowledge intervenes, so jobs lead to increased turnover with the passage of time. This tentative belief is based on 18 formal experimental studies in our first series, and on more than 100 new ones, mostly nonexperimental.

Why does a job get worse? For reasons such as these:

1. A skill within the job is no longer needed; an automatic tool takes over.

2. As problems are solved, the solutions are written and employees are asked to go by the book. The first guy undoubtedly had fun. No, *fun* is not the right concept; I must return to this.

3. Trainers won't let you try a job until you are perfect. Literally, some desirable employees do not stay to finish training. By analogy, golf would not claim many devotees if we could not play on a course until we were perfect.

4. Job simplifiers break up a meaningful slice of work, thus hoping to gain economically (a) by shorter training requirements; (b) by employing people who can be paid less; or (c) by building up enormous skill at a task

that is less and less complex. It is possible, of course, that some jobs are born nude, so utterly simplified that only those with very little ability or a high capacity for fugues or fantasy can tolerate them.

5. By work measurement schemes applied so literally that meaningful and proper exceptions cannot be made. Two examples from a friend employed by an airline: (a) A beautiful sale of $20,000 in tickets resulted in a negative score from the management observer because the agent failed to close the contact with "thank you," as prescribed in the check list, and (b) A counter girl was scored negatively by the observer because she failed to show her teeth when she smiled as a customer stepped up.

A manager has to be very astute to stop this natural downward spiral. The pressure to change will come endlessly from the laboratory, competitors, unions, government, and customers. The boss must ask not only what a proposed job change will do to his customer, his costs, his product, but also what it will do to the relation between his employee and whatever it is that he values from day to day, *in his task*. Worry less about what will happen to the relation between the employee and the boss; that is an effect, not a cause, generally.

This leads to some remarks about the concept of "customer" as used here. When we could give an employee a heightened sense of customer, and responsibility for the customer, we did best with our trials. And, in a sense, there was a customer for everyone in our trial series. The telephone operators, the service representatives, and the installers obviously had customers. But the engineers in one trial did, too; whoever within the company asked for the new facilities on which he had worked was his customer. And so does a keypunch operator have a customer if we are careful. I will use this job as my one example tonight; the rest are written elsewhere.[3]

AN EXAMPLE:
KEY PUNCHING

This job, as most of us know, is a high turnover job. What was done to improve the task? In a trial in Minneapolis, the work of 14 keypunch operators in disbursement accounting was enriched by capitalizing on the fact that employees are indeed different. Some are more experienced, brighter, more responsible in their behavior, etc. Why not give them certain responsibilities commensurate with these facts?

Prior to the study, each girl punched approximately 1/14 of whatever came in for punching that day, as distributed by an assignment clerk. Jobs came and went. The operator met the accuracy and volume requirements set by supervision. Our theory said, don't worry about the relation between her and her supervisor, primarily. Worry about the thinness of her job, that she is merely a "hey-girl" for someone else who has to get out a payroll (the supervisor). Could we increase the clerk's feeling of responsibility, of purpose, by letting *her* get out this payroll, this inventory, or whatever, herself?

The supervisors heard the work theory sketched here, saw some films we've made, and answered some test material designed to sensitize them to the difference between motivation from within a task and attempts to motivate through the surround of the task. Then we started building a list of things we *might* do that *might* give a clerk a stronger feeling of completeness in the transaction between her and "customer."

Customer for a keypunch operator? That was easy: Give this girl the entire plant payroll to punch, when it came in twice a month. All the additions, deletions, changes in pay rates, overtime, etc. Then if the payroll comes out completely right, she is completely right, not 1/14 right. Another expert puncher got the traffic department's payroll; a third got marketing's, etc. Each clerk has 4, 5, or 6 kinds of cards to handle each month. They may get help from each other, and like secretaries proofreading letters, they verify for each other. And would you believe that selected, proven clerks set their own verification rates? Some have earned the right to deal directly with other departments, not through a supervisor. Only 2 out of 14 had earned the right to schedule their own work every day by the end of the trial (10 months), but others were showing such good judgment that this privilege, or responsibility, was due. In short, *all* 14 girls had certain new, clear responsibilities or privileges by the end of the trial, and *some* had earned quite a few unusual ones. And the results as compared to the control unit, which was on a different floor of the same building? Much, much better. It was discovered by the end of the trial that only 10 girls were needed in "experimental." It should be clear that the card assigner was not needed once most of the cards were permanently assigned. The plant department offered the clerk who punched their cards a promotion when an opening occurred. Pregnancy took care of some others, etc. Although another job (that of service representative), with almost nine hundred cases divided between the experimental and control groups, yielded equally good results (see the book), I picked keypunch as an example since so many of you know this job.

It occurs to me that this is truly a transactional episode; we enriched the interchange between employee and "customer," an internal one. The interchange existed before, but only in stunted form. There were transactions previously between clerk and supervisor, or clerk and clerk. They occurred over coffee but they were about dates, clothing, etc. These are not potentially rich as work motivators. Turnover dropped appreciably, as you have probably guessed, and so did absenteeism. It is one matter to be feeling poorly on a day when your own payroll is due to go out, and quite another matter to feel poorly on a day when you are merely one of 14 girls who get that same payroll out.

TOOLS VS. THEORY

As we move into this "work itself" effort, as we call it, the importance of skills in interviewing, questionnaire construction, and sampling recedes. I now see that we loaded an awful burden onto these hardworking tools. We were asking them to deliver to us an idea no one in the group knew, so to speak—the idea that work itself is the basic motivator once the needs or expectations of the employee are reasonably well met. This is the neglected variable; a job must not be viewed as a constant.

I would now say, regarding employee attitude research, that the tools were better than the theory. The former surveys now seem as empty transactionalism, aimed at yielding a pile of data. Now I see the effort as transactionalism with a goal. We want the supervisor to work back and forth with an employee so that every employee ends up with a piece of the business, one that is big enough for him, anyhow.

Many thought the keypunch job was hopeless. But we now have enough evidence to suggest we were wrong. Bear in mind that the clerk is still punching keys, as before, but now she has a complete mission. I trust that you understand me when I say: To punch green cards, then yellow ones, then striped or smelly ones does not meet the objective. Neither does sheer freedom for movement from desk to desk, from punching to verifying, from punching to an adding machine—unless these are natural parts of finishing a job, her job, for the plant department by a specified date.

CERTAIN WEAKNESSES

On the theoretical side, I acknowledge a number of weaknesses. Twenty years and *two* minutes from now I am sure this statement will appear naive. But, I hope, not basically wrong. For we are at last making inroads on dissatisfaction with work. In trials on the service representative's job, with N = 600 in 12 locations, turnover dropped 14 percentage points from a base of 39 per cent, a most pleasing improvement.

Nevertheless, there are some weaknesses:

1. We do not yet adequately understand the great value of work to a human being. Surely it is not a constant; it changes as the society changes.

2. When I present the theory of work and the results, someone always suspects that I disapprove of maintenance factors—money, good human relations, good policies. And some "clever" managers want us to slough off the surrounding items, to offer better jobs for less money, now that we know that people like work. If I could write the regression equation, I would not. But I can't. In some way still not clear to me, I want to

maximize both. This is no zero-sum game, although I suspect we treat it that way when we add money or benefits to offset the natural downward spiral of so many jobs.

3. Work does not have meaning and value for everyone, merely on the average. Employees perform better under this supposition than under the set of assumptions that emphasizes the surround.

4. Even desirable work can be fatiguing; people must be free to leave it when they need to do so. I don't know how to help my company on this problem. I know that "martini logic" does not apply to work either; if one martini makes me feel this good, just think what two or three will do for me!

5. Sooner or later many employees will need to be "re-potted" into bigger jobs if they are to be retained, and I know it. Job enrichment for an individual is not necessarily permanent, but there is a pot somewhere, I suppose, that is big enough for any of us. Things are pretty wishy-washy here. I love Professor Lawrence Peter's theory that all managers rise to their own level of incompetence, where they stay. But I stopped using it when the article came back to me from my boss with the comment, "Why did you send this to me?"

6. The greatest weakness in my current effort to help managers is in the feedback area. I have been subsuming this under the category, "recognition." We handle this poorly, as Richard Farson pointed out in his article, "Praise Reappraised."[4] Praise is hard to give and hard to receive. Somehow—after a while—we management people have got to get out of this part of the transaction. We've got to get it over onto a direct feedback basis. Reinforcement theory and operant conditioning, in general, leave me uneasy where adults are concerned (to any straight psychologists present, I'm sorry about that).

7. We must—and we can—state in better fashion than I have the principles of job enrichment. By principles, I do not mean "chief things." I use principles in the sense, if A then B.

8. I save to last this weakness: our "before versus after" attitude questionnaire is probably a flop despite repeated factorial analyses. In the most conclusive series of studies, where turnover dropped enormously by both corporate standards and by formal tests of statistical significance, the attitude questionnaire said "no change." We don't believe the questionnaire (I'm sorry about that, too). Perhaps job satisfaction is not the right concept. I believe the concept is better connoted by "job involvement." For instance, we observed one of our service representatives crying at her desk because she—all by herself—had deprived a customer of service in error. Under our plan of enrichment, she had earned the right to make such a decision although there was a time when a management person

would have had to concur. In fact, initials from several levels of managers would have been required. I doubt that she was satisfied with herself or the job, but the evidence would suggest that she'll stay on this job longer than a girl who is safe from mistakes. I can assure you that we need her.

Sometimes as I am watching television, I speculate on what I am doing and how I am feeling. "Program satisfaction" would be as poor a descriptive phrase as is job satisfaction. It's program involvement. Am I involved at all in my thinking and feeling with these cowboys and Indians—or whatever—or am I completely passive? If I am involved, I continue. If not, I become a case of channel turnover. "Satisfaction" is quite inadequate obviously, for I watch programs about troubles in the ghetto, on campus, and I watch an occasional who-done-it. Many kinds of programs will involve me. In much the same way, the challenge is to add elements to jobs so that employees can get involved, can make up their own "program" or soap opera for the day.

SHOULD WE BE BOLD

From War Department days until now, never have I felt so certain that research people can be helpful. There has been a real continuity, as I said: soldiers were employees too. I have declared a personal moratorium for five years on all survey studies that aim to find *the one* factor in the job situation which is most important. Go experimental, I suggest, which almost surely will drive you to handling only one variable. So, you've got to specify the variable. If you would help, help us to learn how to handle this neglected variable, *the work itself.* There is a great need—in industry, government, schools, wherever people work for someone else.

RIGHT FOR OUR TIMES

When you elect a president in AAPOR, you automatically confer upon him the right to a mini-modicum of preachment, such as the above. Here is a bit more; then I'll stop. The obstinate employee was (is) trying to tell us something, but he doesn't know what it is. It's not *recognize me,* as implied by the Hawthorne studies, nor *treat me well.* We have tried both of these earnestly from 1940 to date.

The employee is saying, *use me well.* Let my life mean something. More than half of all Americans were not alive in my dear Depression (1930-39), where I learned to panic at the thought of leaving a job. The modern employee in our industrial society, where we have almost no general unemployment, will not respond to a system where we ask him to barter his effort for our benefit plan, a charming place to work, and good manners.

John W. Gardner put it well when he said:

> The release of human potential, the enhancement of individual dignity, the liberation of the human spirit—those are the deepest and truest goals to be conceived by the hearts and minds of the American people. And those are ideas that sustain and strengthen a great civilization—if we believe in them, if we are honest about them, if we have the courage and the stamina to live for them.[5]

Then he goes on to say:

> Of all the ways in which society serves the individual, few are more meaningful than to provide him with a decent job. . . . It isn't going to be a decent society for any of us until it is for all of us. If our sense of responsibility fails us, our sheer self-interest should come to the rescue.[6]

Some people may assume that Gardner was talking about the hardcore unemployed. Actually, he was talking about a just society for all; but in any case, his words amply support the aphorism, "A difference which makes no difference is not different."

A statement of deep truth that appeared at the time of these studies was made by a fellow social psychologist, Kenneth B. Clark, who said:

> The roots of the multiple pathology in the dark ghetto are not easy to isolate. They do not lie primarily in unemployment. In fact, if all of its residents were employed it would not materially alter the pathology of the community. More relevant is the status of the jobs held . . . more important than merely having a job, is the kind of job it is.[7]

You may think that to be an odd switch at the very end of a talk that did not once mention the ghetto problem. If so, forgive me. But we have found not the slightest reason to think our findings on the importance of the wholeness of a piece of work apply only to this group or that one. Both younger and older employees have responded well, as have men and women, blacks and whites, grade school, high school, and college graduates.

So I leave you, I hope, in less of a quandary about this particular obstinate audience—the employee—than when you came in. *Inadequacies in the work itself have been the basis for much of his obstinacy,* not the message about it from management.

REFERENCES

1. *American Psychologist,* Vol. 19, 1964, pp. 319-328.

2. Wiley, New York, 1959.

3. Robert N. Ford, *Motivation through the Work Itself*, New York, American Management Association, 1969.

4. *Harvard Business Review*, September-October 1963.

5. *No Easy Victories*, New York, Harper, 1968, p. 16.

6. *Ibid.*, p. 25.

7. Kenneth B. Clark, "Explosion in the Ghetto," *Psychology Today*, September 1967.

ADDITIONAL READINGS FOR CHAPTER 2

Ford, Robert N., MOTIVATION THROUGH THE WORK ITSELF (New York: American Management Association, Inc., 1969).

Herzberg, Frederick, Mausner, Bernard, and Snyderman, Barbara Bloch, THE MOTIVATION TO WORK, 2nd Ed. (New York: John Wiley and Sons, Inc., 1959).

Herzberg, Frederick, WORK AND THE NATURE OF MAN (Cleveland: The World Publishing Company, 1966).

Chapter 3

ACHIEVEMENT MOTIVATION
AND ORGANIZATIONAL CLIMATE

In his research reported in the last chapter, Herzberg asked various employees to describe, among other things, the sequence of events that occurred when they were exceedingly happy with their jobs. In response to this request, people talked about what they did. They talked about job content, task achievement, recognition for task achievement, responsibility for tasks, and growth and advancement in capability to perform tasks. They did not talk about company policy and administration, supervision, salary, interpersonal relations, and working conditions. Herzberg called the first set of factors, task achievement and so on, motivators because "... other results indicate they are necessary for improvement in performance beyond that pseudo-improvement which in substance amounts to coming up to a 'fair day's work.' " He dismissed the motivational importance of the second set of factors, the hygiene factors, crediting them only with the power to stave off dissatisfactions which might cause a decrease in performance below the level of a fair day's work.

The policy implication of Herzberg's research is straightforward: if managers wish to motivate employees, they must offer them work whose intrinsic content is rich with opportunities to experience feelings of achievement. As Ford put it: "Forget about money, benefits, human relations; let someone else take care of them because that must be done. Dig in exclusively on improving the nature of the job."

Perhaps that is a bit strong. Neither Herzberg nor Ford really mean to forget money. A glance back at the chart in Herzberg's article shows that money is mentioned as a source of satisfaction nearly as often as it is mentioned as a source of dissatisfaction. But when one wishes to emphasize certain implications of research findings, he may understandably leave other results in the background. In any event, Herzberg and Ford assume that work must be changed to meet the nature of man.

But what is the nature of man's needs? Do people want challenging jobs? Do individuals differ markedly in how much they hunger for feelings of achievement? David McClelland points out in the first article in this chapter that, according to his research, only a minority of persons are challenged by opportunity and are willing to work hard to achieve something. The majority really do not care all that much.

If McClelland is correct, then we might do well to tone down any expectations we may have developed for a universal unleashing of talent and energetic commitment to work to follow upon the enrichment of jobs. Just as we have no reason to expect to see people become more productive in response to improved fringe benefits and working conditions, we cannot expect dramatic increases in motivation to occur in most people by offering them jobs with more opportunities for achievement if most people do not care all that much about achievement.

But to be more realistic is not necessarily to be more pessimistic. The fact is that it is not majorities but minorities which account for much of organizational effectiveness. In many kinds of enterprise, 10 percent of the products account for 90 percent of the revenue. Similarly, 10 percent of the salesmen often account for 90 percent of the sales. And 10 percent of the businessmen, the entrepreneurs, account for a surprisingly large percent of economic development.

So minorities are important, especially that minority which tries to make things happen, which is concerned about continual improvement, which sets moderate goals, and which keeps score of its progress and judges it against an internal standard of excellence. This is the minority of persons which David McClelland finds has a high need for achievement (n Ach). His research shows that countries with rapidly growing firms and with relatively more businessmen and managers who have high n Ach have above-average rates of economic growth.

McClelland discusses the nature of achievement motivation and its wider implications. He explains briefly what he has learned about the acquisition of n Ach—how it develops more fully in some people and in some societies than in others. He discusses the relationship of n Ach to economic development.

Additionally, he reports on recent work to help individuals increase their n Ach. Courses were devised to help businessmen do four things: to think and act more like people with high n Ach; to set higher yet realistic work goals for themselves for the next few years; to examine their present behavior to identify values and goals which were determining it; and to work with the sympathy and support of a group undergoing the same experience. McClelland reports that, in some cases, men who took the course made more money, got promoted faster, and expanded their businesses faster than did comparable men who did not take the course. Thus, it appears possible to help individuals develop higher levels of n Ach.

But apart from direct efforts to change the motive strength of *n* Ach in individuals, there are other steps which may be taken to make the environment more conducive to arousal of achievement motivation. In the second article, Robert Stringer explains that managers, by creating the right kind of climate in organizations, ". . . can have a very definite impact on the achievement motivation of their subordinates. They can present those individuals with new sources of satisfaction and new opportunities to achieve, thereby arousing achievement motivation."

Opportunities for arousing achievement motivation, according to Stringer, are plentiful in what might be called the management control system—". . . those processes and structures by which managers assure that resources and energies are put to work serving the objectives of the organization." He stresses setting clearly defined goals which represent moderate risks, adjusting goals as circumstances dictate, evaluating managers in terms of their goal-setting behaviors, providing feedback on progress toward goals, emphasizing individual responsibility, liking rewards consistently with achievements, and providing support and encouragement. Of course, it is the people who are high in *n* Ach who will likely be most responsive to this kind of organizational climate. At the same time, however, this kind of organizational climate can better arouse and develop whatever levels of *n* Ach are present. Such a climate can set in motion a self-reinforcing pattern of activities. As Stringer points out, "Once aroused, achievement-oriented behavior will be self-rewarding."

In reading the articles by McClelland and Stringer, you might consider the following issues: What links do you see between Herzberg's research and McClelland's? What relationship might there be between McGregor's advocacy of decentralization and delegation, job enlargement, participation and consultative management, and performance appraisal methods which stress management by objectives and Stringer's suggestion for management control practices designed to stimulate achievement motivation? What problems do you see in the short course method of achievement training for bringing about lasting behavioral change? Does it seem unequivocally desirable to stimulate *n* Ach generally in an organization?

That Urge
To Achieve

David C. McClelland

Most people in this world, psychologically, can be divided into two broad groups. There is that minority which is challenged by opportunity and willing to work hard to achieve something, and the majority which really does not care all that much.

For nearly twenty years now, psychologists have tried to penetrate the mystery of this curious dichotomy. Is the need to achieve (or the absence of it) an accident, is it hereditary, or is it the result of enrivonment? Is it a single, isolatable human motive, or a combination of motives—the desire to accumulate wealth, power, fame? Most important of all, is there some technique that could give this will to achieve to people, even whole societies, who do not now have it?

While we do not yet have complete answers for any of these questions, years of work have given us partial answers to most of them and insights into all of them. There is a distinct human motive, distinguishable from others. It can be found, in fact tested for, in any group.

Let me give you one example. Several years ago, a careful study was made of 450 workers who had been thrown out of work by a plant shutdown in Erie, Pennsylvania. Most of the unemployed workers stayed home for a while and then checked back with the United States Employment Service to see if their old jobs or similar ones were available. But a small minority among them behaved differently: the day they were laid off, they started job-hunting.

They checked both the United States and the Pennsylvania Employment Office; they studied the "Help Wanted" sections of the papers; they checked through their union, their church, and various fraternal organizations; they looked into training courses to learn a new skill; they even left town to look for

Reprinted by permission from *Think* Magazine, published by IBM, Copyright 1966 by International Business Machines Corporation.

work, while the majority when questioned said they would not under any circumstances move away from Erie to obtain a job. Obviously the members of that active minority were differently motivated. All the men were more or less in the same situation objectively: they needed work, money, food, shelter, job security. Yet only a minority showed initiative and enterprise in finding what they needed. Why? Psychologists, after years of research, now believe they can answer that question. They have demonstrated that these men possessed in greater degree a specific type of human motivation. For the moment let us refer to this personality characteristic as "Motive A" and review some of the other characteristics of the men who have more of the motive than other men.

Suppose they are confronted by a work situation in which they can set their own goals as to how difficult a task they will undertake. In the psychological laboratory, such a situation is very simply created by asking them to throw rings over a peg from any distance they may choose. Most men throw more or less randomly, standing now close, now far away, but those with Motive A seem to calculate carefully where they are most likely to get a sense of mastery. They stand nearly always at moderate distances, not so close as to make the task ridiculously easy, nor so far away as to make it impossible. They set moderately difficult, but potentially achievable goals for themselves, where they objectively have only about a 1-in-3 chance of succeeding. In other words, they are always setting challenges for themselves, tasks to make them stretch themselves a little.

But they behave like this only *if they* can influence the outcome by performing the work themselves. They prefer not to gamble at all. Say they are given a choice between rolling dice with one in three chances of winning and working on a problem with a one-in-three chance of solving in the time allotted, they choose to work on the problem even though rolling the dice is obviously less work and the odds of winning are the same. They prefer to work at a problem rather than leave the outcome to chance or to others.

Obviously they are concerned with personal achievement rather than with the rewards of success *per se*, since they stand just as much chance of getting those rewards by throwing the dice. This leads to another characteristic the Motive A men show—namely, a strong preference for work situations in which they get concrete feedback on how well they are doing, as one does, say in playing golf, or in being a salesman, but as one does not in teaching, or in personnel counseling. A golfer always knows his score and can compare how well he is doing with par or with his own performance yesterday or last week. A teacher has no such concrete feedback on how well he is doing in "getting across" to his students.

THE n ACH MEN

But why do certain men behave like this? At one level the reply is simple: because they habitually spend their time thinking about doing things better. In fact, psychologists typically measure the strength of Motive A by taking samples of a man's spontaneous thoughts (such as making up a story about a picture they have been shown) and counting the frequency with which he mentions doing things better. The count is objective and can even be made these days with the help of a computer program for content analysis. It yields what is referred to technically as an individual's n Ach score (for "need for Achievement"). It is not difficult to understand why people who think constantly about "doing better" are more apt to do better at job-hunting, to set moderate, achievable goals for themselves, to dislike gambling (because they get no achievement satisfaction from success), and to prefer work situations where they can tell easily whether they are improving or not. But why some people and not others come to think this way is another question. The evidence suggests it is not because they are born that way, but because of special training they get in the home from parents who set moderately high achievement goals but who are warm, encouraging and nonauthoritarian in helping their children reach these goals.

Such detailed knowledge about one motive helps correct a lot of common sense ideas about human motivation. For example, much public policy (and much business policy) is based on the simpleminded notion that people will work harder "if they have to." As a first approximation, the idea isn't totally wrong, but it is only a half-truth. The majority of unemployed workers in Erie "had to" find work as much as those with higher n Ach, but they certainly didn't work as hard at it. Or again, it is frequently assumed that any strong motive will lead to doing things better. Wouldn't it be fair to say that most of the Erie workers were just "unmotivated"? But our detailed knowledge of various human motives shows that each one leads a person to behave in different ways. The contrast is not between being "motivated" or "unmotivated" but between being motivated toward A or toward B or C, etc.

A simple experiment makes the point nicely: subjects were told that they could choose as a working partner either a close friend or a stranger who was known to be an expert on the problem to be solved. Those with higher n Ach (more "need to achieve") chose the experts over their friends, whereas those with more n Aff (the "need to affiliate with others") chose friends over experts. The latter were not "unmotivated"; their desire to be with someone they liked was simply a stronger motive than their desire to excel at the task. Other such needs have been studied by psychologists. For instance, the need for Power is often confused with the need for Achievement because both may lead to "outstanding" activities. There is a distinct difference. People with a strong need for Power want to command attention, get recognition, and control others. They are more active in political life and tend to busy themselves primarily with controlling the channels of communication both up to the top and down to the people so that they are more "in charge." Those with high n Power are not as concerned with improving their work performance daily as those with high n Ach.

It follows, from what we have been able to learn, that not all "great achievers" score high in n Ach. Many generals, outstanding politicians, great research scientists do not, for instance, because their work requires other personality characteristics, other motives. A general or a politician must be more concerned with power relationships, a research scientist must be able to go for long periods without the immediate feedback the person with high n Ach requires, etc. On the other hand, business executives, particularly if they are in positions of real responsibility or if they are salesmen, tend to score high in n Ach. This is true even in a Communist country like Poland: apparently there, as well as in a private enterprise economy, a manager succeeds if he is concerned about improving all the time, setting moderate goals, keeping track of his or the company's performance, etc.

MOTIVATION AND HALF-TRUTHS

Since careful study has shown that common sense notions about motivation are at best half-truths, it also follows that you cannot trust what people tell you about their motives. After all, they often get their ideas about their own motives from common sense. Thus a general may say he is interested in achievement (because he has obviously achieved), or a businessman that he is interested only in making money (because he has made money), or one of the majority of unemployed in Erie that he desperately wants a job (because he knows he needs one); but a careful check of what each one thinks about and how he spends his time may show that each is concerned about quite different things. It requires special measurement techniques to identify the presense of n Ach and other such motives. Thus what people say and believe is not very closely related to these "hidden" motives which seem to affect a person's "style of life" more than his political, religious or social attitudes. Thus n Ach produces enterprising men among labor leaders or managers, Republicans or Democrats, Catholics or Protestants, capitalists or Communists.

Wherever people begin to think often in n Ach terms, things begin to move. Men with higher n Ach get more raises and are promoted more rapidly, because they keep actively seeking ways to do a better job. Companies with many such men grow faster. In one comparison of two firms in Mexico, it was discovered that all but one of the top executives of a fast growing firm had higher n Ach scores than the highest scoring executive in an equally large but slow-growing firm. Countries with many such rapidly growing firms tend to show above-average rates of economic growth. This appears to be the reason why correlations have regularly been found between the n Ach content in popular literature (such as popular songs or stories in children's textbooks) and subsequent rates of national economic growth. A nation which is thinking about doing better all the time (as shown in its popular literature) actually does do better economically speaking. Careful quantitative studies have shown this to be true in Ancient Greece, in Spain in the Middle Ages, in England from 1400-1800, as well as among contemporary nations, whether capitalist or Communist, developed or underdeveloped.

Contrast these two stories for example. Which one contains more *n* Ach? Which one reflects a state of mind which ought to lead to harder striving to improve the way things are:

Excerpt from story A (4th grade reader): "Don't Ever Owe a Man—The world is an illusion. Wife, children, horses and cows are all just ties of fate. They are ephemeral. Each after fulfilling his part in life disappears. So we should not clamour after riches which are not permanent. As long as we live it is wise not to have any attachments and just think of God. We have to spend our lives without trouble, for is it not time that there is an end to grievances? So it is better to live knowing the real state of affairs. Don't get entangled in the meshes of family life."

Excerpt from story B (4th grade reader): "How I Do Like to Learn—I was sent to an accelerated technical high school. I was so happy I cried. Learning is not very easy. In the beginning I couldn't understand what the teacher taught us. I always got a red cross mark on my papers. The boy sitting next to me was very enthusiastic and also an outstanding student. When he found I couldn't do the problems he offered to show me how he had done them. I could not copy his work. I must learn through my own reasoning. I gave his paper back and explained I had to do it myself. Sometimes I worked on a problem until midnight. If I couldn't finish, I started early in the morning. The red cross marks on my work were getting less common. I conquered my difficulties. My marks rose. I graduated and went on to college."

Most readers would agree, without any special knowledge of the *n* Ach coding system, that the second story shows more concern with improvement than the first, which comes from a contemporary reader used in Indian public schools. In fact the latter has a certain Horatio Alger quality that is reminiscent of our own McGuffey readers of several generations ago. It appears today in the textbooks of Communist China. It should not, therefore, come as a surprise if a nation like China, obsessed as it is with improvement, tended in the long run to outproduce a nation like India, which appears to be more fatalistic.

The *n* Ach level is obviously important for statesmen to watch and in many instances to try to do something about, particularly if a nation's economy is lagging. Take Britain, for example. A generation ago (around 1925) it ranked fifth among 25 countries where children's readers were scored for *n* Ach—and its economy was doing well. By 1950 the *n* Ach level had dropped to 27th out of 39 countries—well below the world average—and today, its leaders are feeling the severe economic effects of this loss in the spirit of enterprise.

ECONOMICS AND n ACH

If psychologists can detect *n* Ach levels in individuals or nations, particularly before their effects are widespread, can't the knowledge somehow be put to use to foster economic development? Obviously detection or diagnosis is not enough. What good is it to tell Britain (or India for that matter) that it needs more *n* Ach, a greater spirit of enterprise? In most such cases, informed observers of the local scene know very well that such a need exists, though they may be slower to discover it than the psychologist hovering over *n* Ach scores. What is needed is some method of developing *n* Ach in individuals or nations.

Since about 1960, psychologists in my research group at Harvard have been experimenting with techniques designed to accomplish this goal, chiefly among business executives whose work requires the action characteristics of people with high *n* Ach. Initially, we had real doubts as to whether we could succeed, partly because like most American psychologists we had been strongly influenced by the psychoanalytic view that basic motives are laid down in childhood and cannot really be changed later, and partly because many studies of intensive psycho-therapy and counseling have shown minor if any long-term personality effects. On the other hand we were encouraged by the nonprofessionals: those enthusiasts like Dale Carnegie, the Communist ideologue or the Church missionary, who felt they could change adults and in fact seemed to be doing so. At any rate we ran some brief (7 to 10 days) "total push" training courses for businessmen, designed to increase their *n* Ach.

FOUR MAIN GOALS

In broad outline the courses had four main goals: (1) They were designed to teach the participants how to think, talk and act like a person with high *n* Ach, based on our knowledge of such people gained through 17 years of research. For instance, men learned how to make up stories that would code high in *n* Ach (i.e., how to think in *n* Ach terms), how to set moderate goals for themselves in the ring toss game (and in life). (2) The courses stimulated the participants to set higher but carefully planned and realistic work goals for themselves over the next two years. Then we checked back with them every six months to see how well they were doing in terms of their own objectives. (3) The courses also utilized techniques for giving the participants knowledge about themselves. For instance, in playing the ring toss game, they could observe that they behaved differently from others—perhaps in refusing to adjust a goal downward after failure. This would then become a matter for group discussion and the man would have to explain what he had in mind in setting such unrealistic goals. Discussion could then lead on to what a man's ultimate goals in life were, how much he cared about actually improving performance v. making a good impression or having many friends. In this way the participants would be freer to realize their achievement goals without being blocked by old habits and attitudes. (4) The courses also usually created a group *esprit de corps* from learning about each other's hopes and fears, successes and failures, and from going through an emotional experience together, away from everyday life, in a retreat setting. This membership in a new group helps a man achieve his goals, partly because he knows he has their sympathy and support and partly because he knows they will be watching to see how well he does. The same effect has been noted in other therapy groups like Alcoholics Anonymous. We are not sure which of these course "inputs" is really absolutely essential—that remains a research question—but we are taking no chances at the outset in view of the general pessimism about such efforts, and we wanted to include any and all techniques that were thought to change people.

The courses have been given: to executives in a large American firm, and in several Mexican firms; to underachieving high school boys; and to businessmen in India from Bombay and from a small city—Kakinada in the state of Andhra Pradesh. In every instance save one (the Mexican case), it was possible to demonstrate statistically, some two years later, that the men who took the course had done better (made more money, got promoted faster, expanded their businesses faster) than comparable men who did not take the course or who took some other management course.

Consider the Kakinada results, for example. In the two years preceding the course 9 men, 18 percent of the 52 participants, had shown "unusual" enterprise in their businesses. In the 18 months following the course 25 of the men, in other words nearly 50 percent, were unusually active. And this was not due to a general upturn of business in India. Data from a control city, some forty-five miles away, show the same base rate of "unusually active" men as in Kakinada before the course—namely, about 20 percent. Something clearly happened in Kakinada: the owner of the small radio shop started a chemical plant; a banker was so successful in making commercial loans in an enterprising way that he was promoted to a much larger branch of his bank in Calcutta; the local political leader accomplished his goal (it was set in the course) to get the federal government to deepen the harbor and make it into an all-weather port; plans are far along for establishing a steel rolling mill, etc. All this took place without any substantial capital input from the outside. In fact, the only costs were for four 10-day courses plus some brief follow-up visits every six months. The men are raising their own capital and using their own resources for getting business and industry moving in a city that had been considered stagnant and unenterprising.

The promise of such a method of developing achievement motivation seems very great. It has obvious applications in helping underdeveloped countries, or "pockets of poverty" in the United States, to move faster economically. It has great potential for businesses that need to "turn around" and take a more enterprising approach toward their growth and development. It may even be helpful in developing more *n* Ach among low-income groups. For instance, data show that lower-class Negro Americans have a very low level of *n* Ach. This is not surprising. Society has systematically discouraged and blocked their achievement striving. But as the barriers to upward mobility are broken down, it will be necessary to help stimulate the motivation that will lead them to take advantage of new opportunities opening up.

EXTREME REACTIONS

But a word of caution: Whenever I speak of this research and its great potential, audience reaction tends to go to opposite extremes. Either people remain skeptical and argue that motives can't really be changed, that all we are doing is dressing Dale Carnegie up in fancy "psychologese," or they become converts and want instant course descriptions by return mail to solve their local motivational problems. Either response is unjustified. What I have described here in a few pages has taken 20 years of patient research effort, and hundreds of thousands of dollars in basic research costs. What remains to be done will involve even larger sums and more time for development to turn a promising idea into something of wide practical utility.

ENCOURAGEMENT NEEDED

To take only one example, we have not yet learned how to develop *n* Ach really well among low-income groups. In our first effort—a summer course for bright underachieving 14-year-olds—we found that boys from the middle class improved steadily in grades in school over a two-year period, but boys from the lower class showed an improvement after the first year followed by a drop back to their beginning low grade average. (See chart at right.) Why? We speculated that it was because they moved back into an environment in which neither parents nor friends encouraged achievement or upward mobility. In other words, it isn't enough to change a man's motivation if the environment in which he lives doesn't support at least to some degree his new efforts. Negroes striving to rise out of the ghetto frequently confront this problem: they are often faced by skepticism at home and suspicion on the job, so that even if their *n* Ach is raised, it can be lowered again by the heavy odds against their success. We must learn not only to raise *n* Ach but also to find methods of instructing people in how to manage it, to create a favorable environment in which it can flourish.

Many of these training techniques are now only in the pilot testing stage. It will take time and money to perfect them, but society should be willing to invest heavily in them in view of their tremendous potential for contributing to human betterment.

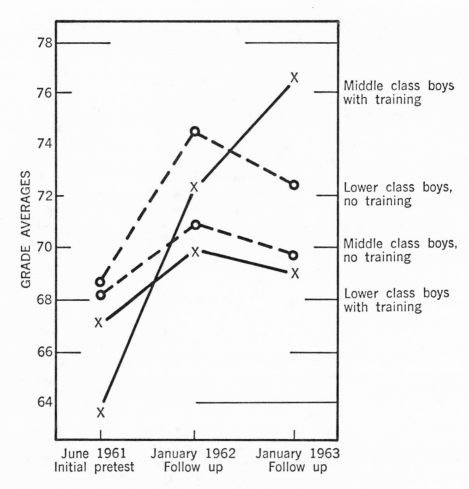

Figure 1. *In a Harvard study, a group of underachieving
14-year-olds was given a six-week course designed to help them
do better in school. Some of the boys were also given training
in achievement motivation or n Ach (solid lines).
As graph reveals, the only boys who continued
to improve after a two-year period were the middle-class
boys with the special n Ach training. Psychologists suspect
the lower-class boys dropped back, even with n Ach training,
because they returned to an environment in which neither parents
nor friends encouraged achievement.*

Achievement Motivation
and Management Control

Robert A. Stringer, Jr.

Most adults carry around with them the potential energy to behave in a variety of ways. Whether or not they do behave in these ways depends on (1) the kinds of motives or needs a person has, and (2) the characteristics of the environment.

A person's motivation is said to depend on three factors. First, the "basic" strength of the particular motive; second, the person's expectation that he can satisfy the motive in this situation; and third, the amount of satisfaction the person anticipates.

The final two determinants of aroused motivation are not part of a person's personality. They are not inside the person. They can be considered characteristics of the environment, because they change as the person moves from situation to situation. Different work settings signal to the individual that different kinds of satisfactions can be gained by behaving in certain ways. These signals (or cues) lead to different kinds of motivation. By understanding the varieties of human motivation, managers will be in a better position to control the activities of their subordinates.

It is assumed that every individual personality is composed of a network of these basic motives. Some of the more important motives that have been studied are:

Need for Achievement: the need for competitive success as measured against some standard of excellence;

Need for Power: the need for personal influence and control over the means of influencing others;

Need for Affiliation: the need for close interpersonal relationships and friendships;

Fear of Failure: the fear of competition or criticism when involved in an activity that is to be evaluated.

Motives are generally acquired during a person's early years, and they remain relatively unchanged in adult life. *Motivation,* however, is determined by the interplay between a person and his environment. Thus a man's *motivated behavior* may change radically throughout his adult life.

ACHIEVEMENT MOTIVATION

Managers must concern themselves with *motivation to accomplish results.* When a man's motivation to achieve is aroused, accomplishment of the task will be its own best reward. The significance of achievement motivation revolves around this notion of self-reinforcing performance. When we speak of "self-motivated" men, we refer to men who are acting to satisfy their need to achieve.

It is not surprising that McClelland found high levels of achievement motivation associated with entrepreneurial behavior, innovative risk-taking, and business success.[1] Men with a high need to achieve ("high achievers") tend to:

1. seek and assume high degrees of personal responsibility,

2. take calculated risks,

3. set challenging, but realistic goals for themselves,

4. develop comprehensive plans to help them attain their goals,

5. seek and use concrete, measurable feedback of the results of their actions, and

6. seek out business opportunities where their desires to achieve will not be thwarted.

McClelland has also pointed out that environmental factors greatly influence achievement motivation.[2] This, of course, is consistent with our principles of motivation. But what are the critical dimensions of the environment that influence motivation to achieve? Recent research has sought to answer this question.[3] The implications of this research, although tentative, seem clear. High achievers will be attracted to those business environments which offer:

1. personal responsibility for accomplishments,
2. freedom to pursue goals by means of one's own choosing,
3. prompt and unbiased feedback of the results of action,
4. moderately risky situations, and
5. consistent rewards and recognition for jobs well done.

These climactic factors seem to stimulate achievement motivation in the individual. They add up to excitement and satisfaction.

CLIMATE AND CONTROL

By creating the right kind of climate, managers can have a very definite impact on the achievement motivation of their subordinates. They can present these individuals with new sources of satisfaction and new opportunities to achieve, thereby arousing achievement motivation. Once aroused, achievement-oriented behavior will be self-rewarding. Thus, the manager need not exercise constant and forceful restraint on his subordinte's activities.

An important tool in the hands of management to influence the climate of their organizations and the motivation of their subordinates is the management control system. We will define control systems as those processes and structures by which managers assure that resources and energies are put to work serving the objectives of the organization.

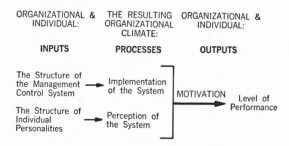

Exhibit 1

Every individual interprets or perceives the control system differently, and therefore the concept of "organizational climate" is needed. When we speak of environmental influences on human motivation, we are referring to the perceived environment; that is, the climate. (*See Exhibit 1.*)

Climate is determined by the structure *and* the implementation of the control system, and the values and attitudes that each manager brings to the job of control. For example, the managers in Division A might be sticklers for detail and insist on following the prescribed control procedures exactly. Managers in

Division B, operating under a very similar structure, may choose to ignore a lot of the detailed rules or procedures. In this kind of organization, the two divisions may perform very differently. Why? The answers, on the surface, seem to be obvious. "People in Division A resent all the rules and regulations." Or, "Division B performs well because the workers are 'motivated' to do a better job."

Such explanations do not help the manager do his job better. Such explanations describe, rather than analyze, the causal factors involved. Analysis requires understanding. This article aims to provide a basis for better understanding of the dynamics of human motivation in work situations. We will present eight propositions about motivation to achieve.

It is assumed that there is a certain "base level" of motivation to achieve operative at the present time, but that the full potential of this achievement motivation is going unrealized. The basic strategy of these eight propositions is to program the management control processes in such a way that achievement-oriented behavior is reinforced and rewarded.

Proposition 1: *Achievement motivation will tend to be aroused if the goals of the responsibility center are made explicit.*

Achievement motivation, by definition, refers to competition with a standard of excellence. This standard may be internal (within the individual's own mind) or external (stated by the organization within which he works). By making external performance standards explicit, individuals can include them in their internal frame of reference. The specific goals and objectives of the responsibility center can become part of each individual's future plans. Personal achievement can be defined in terms of the yardsticks and measurements which are most important to the organization. That is, if quality is less important than pure volume, it would be dysfunctional for workers to strive for 100%-perfect quality. By making the quality standards explicit—both as to the specific level *and* the relative importance of other goals—achievement energies can be channeled into more useful pursuits.

Proposition 2: *Achievement motivation will tend to be aroused if goals represent a moderate degree of risk for the individuals involved.*

Individuals with high motivation prefer to work under conditions of moderate risk. That is, the subjective probabilities of success should be about 50-50. If goals seem to be speculative and the likelihood of success is very low, motivation to achieve will not be aroused. If the goals are too conservative and the likelihood of success if quite high, motivation will not be aroused. Moderately risky goals represent a continuing challenge, and it is this element of challenge that must be stated in the goals of the responsibility center and the goals of the individual.

Several alternatives are open to the manager in implementing this proposition. He may assess the chances of success and failure for his subordinates and impose a goal that, in his mind, seems like a moderately risky one. Or he may rely on his subordinate's judgment and opinion, and allow the subordinate some freedom in setting his goals. (*See Exhibit 2.*)

Proposition 3:   *A higher level of achievement motivation will tend to be aroused if provision is made in the management control process for adjusting specific goals when the chances of goal-accomplishment change significantly (from the 50-50 level).*

The facts of business life are clear: environments are continally changing, and the chances of success change with each change in the environment. Even without any significant change in the environment, the odds of success may change as additional information about the tasks and the critical skills become known. A calculated risk in January may become an impossible goal by May.

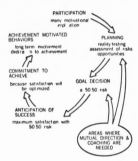

Exhibit 2

To achieve flexibility, there are at least two alternatives open to management. First, the formal reward system could be adjusted to account for the risk elements of performance. Subordinates who succeeded in accomplishing goals that were judged to be 50-50 risks could be paid more than subordinates who worked toward conservative or speculative goals. A second alternative could be to have a provision for systematic review and adjustment of goals when the odds of success deviate significantly from the 50-50 criteria.

The second alternative is the most desirable. By providing for changes in individual and responsibility center goals, the control process will be facilitating the development of achievement motivation. By forcing managers and their subordinates to examine their objectives and by insisting that these objectives remain challenging (that is, with 50-50 odds of accomplishment), the entire climate of the organization can be injected with new excitement and achievement.

Proposition 4:   *Achievement motivation will tend to be aroused if managers are evaluated in terms of their goal setting behaviors.*

Because of the central importance of goal-setting, the creation of an achieving climate will be furthered by zeroing in on this activity when evaluating individual managers.

We are not suggesting that managers be rewarded in proportion to their *performance* compared to the degree of risk (this idea was rejected in 3). Rather, we are suggesting that they be rewarded for setting moderately risky goals.

Proposition 5: *Achievement motivation will tend to be aroused if individuals are given feedback of the progress they are making toward their goals.*

Empirical research has found that high achievers characteristically desire concrete feedback of the results of their actions. This feedback not only gives them achievement satisfaction, but it helps them plan ahead and set more realistic goals in the future. Further proof of this point is that high achievers tend to *seek* jobs which provide for immediate and tangible feedback, such as sales positions.

Several aspects of performance feedback are especially important. It should be: (a) prompt, (b) unbiased, and (c) relevant. The implications of these aspects of the feedback process on management control are far-reaching.

When feedback of performance is given only pertinent information should be used. A wealth of data tends to confuse, rather than motivate, managers. One successful attempt to solve this problem involves the extensive use of graphic presentations.

Proposition 6: *Achievement motivation will tend to be aroused if there is a climate that emphasizes individual responsibility.*

High achievers seek success, and unless they can plainly see that their success is truly theirs, little achievement satisfaction can be gained. To increase the opportunity for achievement satisfactions, the organization must place a premium on the assumption of personal responsibility at all levels of management.

In both the goal-setting and performance review processes, a climate of responsibility will be created if (1) there is a "results orientation" and (2) there is sufficient "coaching." By focusing on the desired results, the entire achievement syndrome is forced upon the manager, for a *results orientation focuses on those aspects of the subordinate's behavior which are critical to his personal achievement and the achievement of the firm.* Other issues will be placed in secondary positions.

Proposition 7: *Achievement motivation will be aroused if the rewards and punishments formally provided for as part of the management control system are perceived as consistent with achievement goals.*

One consequence of the development of high levels of achievement motivation is that achievement itself becomes the most important reward. High achievers derive most of their satisfaction out of doing a good job, not out of receiving the external rewards associated with success. Formal organizational rewards are important, however, for they satisfy other personal needs and they may *symbolize success*. Thus, careful control of organizational rewards and punishments may be useful in arousing achievement.

Researchers have found that high achievers *expect to be punished* when they fail to achieve their goals. Such expectations seem to make success all the more satisfying. If organizations fail to discriminate between success and failure, or if punishments are not associated with failure to accomplish results, the entire reward system will have relatively little effect on achievement.

The fourth consideration raises important theoretical and practical questions. Rewards and punishments should be dispensed to individuals, not to groups or responsibility centers.

When rewards are given to groups rather than to individuals, personal accomplishments may be buried, making it difficult to arouse entrepreneurial spirit. A formal reward system built around individual rewards for individual accomplishments is more consistent with the six preceding propositions.

Proposition 8:   *Achievement motivation will tend to be increased when there is a climate of mutual support and encouragement.*

The theoretical support for this proposition goes beyond the relatively simple concepts of achievement motivation that have been presented earlier. Briefly, it has been found that the motive, Fear of Failure (or Need To Avoid Failure), debilitates motivation to achieve. A high level of the failure motive will proportionately weaken the resultant achievement motivation.

The creation of a supportive climate tends to reduce anxiety and negate many of the dysfunctional effects that anxiety is likely to have on continued high performance. To stimulate achievement motivation, support must be task-oriented. If task-related support and encouragement is stressed, the entire organizational climate can become "self-generating." That is, *mutual support* will act as a powerful reinforcement device. Coaching, helping, informal encouragements, and other reciprocal supportive relationships can solidify the arousal effects of propositions 1 through 7.

SUMMARY

Arousal of achievement motivation is desirable *when there is an entrepreneurial function to be performed*. When risks must be taken, when specific objectives must be set and met, and when individuals must act on their own initiative and live with their results, the proper framework for control revolves around these eight propositions.

The ultimate responsibility for implementation of these new management control processes must lie with line managers. Control personnel can describe and initiate the framework, but they cannot create the on-going working climate that is required. If management succeeds in altering the climate and management control processes, what can be expected? If motivation is aroused and if achievement successes begin to reinforce this arousal, a new spirit of dynamic growth can be fostered. With growth will come new challenges and new risks. But the high achiever can be a selfish soul. Once he tastes success, his appetite is nearly insatiable. Unless the firm can continue to present him with challenges and responsibility, he may seek them elsewhere.

REFERENCES

1. McClelland, D.C., *The Achieving Society*, Van Nostrand, Princeton, N.J. 1961.

2. —————, "Toward a Theory of Motive Acquisition," in *American Psychologist*, May 1965; "Achievement Motivation Can Be Developed," *Harvard Business Review*, Nov-Dec. 1965.

3. Litwin, G. H. & Stringer, R. A., *Motivation and Organizational Climate*, Harvard Graduate School of Business Administration Division of Research (in process); *The Influence of Organizational Climate on Human Motivation*, unpublished monograph, 1966.

ADDITIONAL READINGS FOR CHAPTER 3

Atkinson, John W. (ed.), MOTIVES IN FANTASY, ACTION, AND SOCIETY (Princeton: D. Van Nostrand Company, Inc., 1958).

—————————, AN INTRODUCTION TO MOTIVATION (New York: American Book Company, 1964).

Litwin, George H. and Robert A. Stringer, Jr., MOTIVATION AND ORGANIZATIONAL CLIMATE (Boston: Division of Research, Graduate School of Business Administration, Harvard University, 1968).

McClelland, David C., THE ACHIEVING SOCIETY (Princeton: D. Van Nostrand Company, Inc., 1969).

McClelland, David C. and David G. Winter, MOTIVATING ECONOMIC ACHIEVEMENT (New York: The Free Press, 1969).

Patchen, Martin, PARTICIPATION, ACHIEVEMENT, AND INVOLVEMENT ON THE JOB (Englewood Cliffs, New Jersey: Prentice-Hall, Inc., 1970).

Chapter 4

REWARDS
AND PERFORMANCE

The theorists we have studied so far have not given much prominence to money as a motivator. If they have not ignored the role of the financial incentive, they also have not given it explicit and extended analysis. For Herzberg, money is good for avoiding states of dissatisfaction. For McGregor, money seems capable of satisfying only lower-level needs, needs which he evidently does not see operating as very important motivational opportunities in modern organizations. For Stringer, "One consequence of the development of high levels of achievement motivation is that achievement itself becomes the most important reward. High achievers derive most of their satisfaction out of doing a good job, not out of receiving the external rewards associated with success." He does go on to say that, "Formal organizational rewards are important, however, for they satisfy other personal needs and they may *symbolize success.*"

These comments reflect the tendency of modern behavioral theory to give work itself, not money, the prominent role in motivation. Certainly this new emphasis corrects for a neglect in the past. But at the same time, the theories may have understated the role of money in motivation.

Money is a reward, and behavior is a function of rewards. How rewards determine behavior is expressed by the value and success propositions of behavioral psychology:

> 1. Men are more likely to perform an activity, the more valuable they perceive the reward of that activity to be.

[1] George C. Homans, "Bringing Men Back In," *American Sociological Review,* 20 (December 1964), 816. For a fuller discussion of these ideas, see B. Berelson and G. Steiner, *Human Behavior* (New York: Harcourt, Brace & World, 1964), pp. 133-237; also G. C. Homans, *Social Behavior* (New York: Harcourt, Brace & World, 1961), pp. 30-82.

2. Men are more likely to perform an activity, the more successful they perceive the activity is likely to be in getting that reward.[1]

The rewards must be perceived as valuable, and the efforts to achieve them must be seen as likely to be successful in getting the reward.

The problem for management is to create links between rewards and performance, to foster expectations that efforts will result in performance and that performance will result in rewards. Of course, what a manager thinks will be valued by employees may not be, in fact, what employees do value. Employees may not value pay increases and fringe benefits in the way managers think they do. Money may not be perceived by employees as a reward contingent upon performance, but a reward obtained merely by participation. If this condition exists, money will not be effective in motivating performance. As McGregor pointed out, managers are often puzzled by the failure of wages and fringe benefits to motivate.

We need not conclude from this failure that money is incapable of motivating. The lesson may be that managers have not learned to use money as a motivator. They may not have been effective in linking rewards and performance, in making money contingent upon performance.

The articles in this chapter question management's skillfulness in using money as a motivator. They reexamine assumptions and past practices and recommend new approaches to linking money and performance. In the first article, Victor Vroom analyzes three managerial strategies for motivating people. The first, the paternalistic strategy, resembles the one McGregor discussed, where the manager assumes that people will work effectively out of feelings of gratitude and loyalty. Such feelings will develop in reciprocity for having been paid well and given good benefits and working conditions. But since such rewards are obtained for merely being employed by the organization, they do little to encourage more than the decision to be employed. They encourage membership or participation, but they don't seem to encourage effective performance.

Second, the scientific management strategy utilizes rewards but associates them with, and makes them conditional upon, effective performance. The idea is to make everyone resemble the entrepreneur, in that pay is directly tied to accomplishment. The corollary is that just as rewards follow desired behavior, punishment—warnings, discipline, discharge—follows undesired behavior. The system is somewhat easier to describe than to operate, however. It isn't always practicable to isolate the effects of one person's action in a complex system of interdependent performances. But the scheme has a good foundation in psychological theory, and, where the outcomes of performance can be identified and can be under an individual's control, the scientific management strategy has played and will continue to play a part in stimulating individuals to effective performance.

Third, the participative management strategy operates on the assumption that conditions can be created so that people can satisfy various needs by doing an effective job *per se.* This is the idea which has been given most attention by the authors who have preceded Vroom in this volume. Vroom points out the great merits of the participative approach but stresses the importance of integrating it with the scientific management strategy to capitalize on the power of each.

The second article, by Edward Lawler, does not represent an application of Vroom's concepts but an original development of related and compatible ideas. Lawler stresses the role of perception in motivation. "Rewards must be perceived to be important and obtainable as a result of good job performance." Pay cannot motivate performance, according to Lawler, unless it is perceived as important and contingent upon performance.

Lawler makes use of Maslow's hierarchy-of-needs theory and suggests that pay derives its particular importance through its capacity in modern society to contribute to the satisfaction of needs for esteem and recognition. Since society influences, to some extent, the perception of pay as important, management in a given organization cannot altogether control the importance of pay. But it can affect perceptions about pay in a number of ways. For example, by making salaries known rather than keeping them secret, management can encourage realistic comparisons. The success of some and the lack of success of others can be visible.

Organizations have more control over the link between rewards and performance than over the perceived importance of pay. Management can create large differences between the pay raises given to good and poor performers, thereby nurturing the belief that pay is contingent upon performance. When people see that good work by others is rewarded, they will expect that it will be rewarded in their own cases.

The third article, by Saul Gellerman, develops the thesis that more effective use of money can be made to stimulate performance. He reiterates the point that money often does nothing more than achieve the result of keeping the employee in the organization. Small periodic increases and compressed corporate salary scales do little more than keep pace with the periodic expectation of an increase in earnings.

Gellerman offers a number of specific recommendations for more effective compensation administration. He advocates bigger differences in pay between star performers and ordinary performers. He argues that executives would perform better if their pay were *not* linked to the organization's fortunes. Men who are not afraid to think independently, men who work because they want to, according to Gellerman, can be more credible. They can advocate what they believe is right without fear of retribution. But they can do this only if the rewards system makes them financially independent.

As you read Vroom, Lawler, and Gellerman, you might consider the following questions: What control and leadership practices would seem to support the effective use of money as a motivator? What problems might be associated with making known everyone's pay in an organization? How might emphasis upon individual rewards affect cooperation? What role has motivation to earn money played in your own behavior? What might the motivational effects be if a job was well paid but lacked a participative role as defined by Vroom? What might the motivational effects be if a job had abundant participative qualities but was underpaid? What would be the motivational effects if efforts and achievements on the job did not seem to have any connection with how much one was paid within the rate range on the job? If it is important to link rewards and perform- ance, why is seniority alone so often the determinant of pay? What points of agreement and what points of disagreement do you see in the ideas of Lawler and Gellerman?

The Role
Of Compensation
In Motivating Employees

Victor H. Vroom

For a long time, compensation and the issues which surround it received little attention from behavioral scientists. The important research problems of the 1940s and 1950s involved the effects of supervisory behavior and work group characteristics on individual behavior and productivity. Company executives could read in the writings of behavioral scientists about how appraisal interviews should be conducted, about when groups should be used in making decisions, about the best relationship between staff and line, etc., but could receive little guidance in making compensation decisions or in formulating compensation policy. In the absence of sound data on the consequences of different compensation systems, they were forced to rely for decision making on surveys about what other companies were doing. This undoubtedly had the effect of decreasing the variance in corporate practices but it is doubtful that it contributed significantly either to collective understanding concerning the processes underlying the effects of compensation systems on people or to the rational design of compensation systems.

Fortunately, there are indications that the deficiencies in research which characterized the 1940s and 50s are being remedied in the 1960s. More and more behavioral scientists, particularly the younger representatives of their disciplines, are directing their research efforts toward issues and problems in the area of compensation. There appear to me to be three organizational strategies for motivating their members. Certainly, most companies utilize all three, sometimes at different levels in the hierarchy; however, I think that keeping the three separate will help to bring into focus the issues involved in compensation.

From a talk delivered at the annual conference of the Life Office Management Association. Reprinted by permission of the author and the publisher from *Best's Insurance News*, (Life Ed.), Vol. 67, No. 12 (April, 1967), 67-74.

The first of these answers or organizational strategies for motivation can be called a paternalistic theory. It assumes that people dislike work but can be made to work effectively out of a feeling of gratitude to the organization. It is based on the assumption that if workers are rewarded they will work harder. The more their needs are satisfied the greater the extent to which they will respond with gratitude and loyalty by producing effectively on their jobs.

The essence of this approach is to make the company a source of important rewards—rewards for which the only qualification is employment within the company. In other words, the rewards which are utilized in this theory may be termed unconditional rewards. The amount of reward that any individual receives is not dependent in any way on how he behaves within the organization but rather on the fact that he is a member of that organization.

Some of the practices and programs within organizations which are consistent with this paternalistic view are the various forms of indirect compensation—things like pension plans, group insurance, free medical care, subsidized education programs, and the like. Also qualifying are employee clubs, recreation programs, the company golf course, attractive and comfortable working conditions, subsidized meals, and pleasant cafeterias. One might also add to this list high wage levels, across the board wage increases, implicit or explicit assurance of job security, paying the job and not the man, and promotion on the basis of seniority rather than merit.

How would a manager behave so as to be consistent with the paternalistic approach? He would seek to arrange conditions of work so that his people would feel comfortable, happy, and secure. His primary goal is to see to it that his subordinates are able to get the things they want and he assumes, as a consequence of this support, that his subordinates will display enthusiasm and loyalty. He would try to make his unit one big happy family and to avoid disagreement and conflict.

The one common property of all these rewards is that they are attractive and valued by individual employees—in that sense they are rewards—but none of them are allocated on the basis of differential effort and performance within the organization. As long as one retains his membership in the organization he receives these rewards. The moment he relinquishes his membership, he ceases to receive them.

REWARDS ARE EFFECTIVE

These unconditional rewards have proven to be quite effective in attracting people into organizations. There is no doubt that a company with high wage levels, good fringe benefits, and pleasant working conditions is in a better competitive position to recruit personnel than one with lower wage levels, less liberal fringes, and less pleasant working conditions. It is quite possible, however, that paternalistic practices have some less desirable effects on the type of persons that are recruited. I know of one large corporation that has been making concentrated effort to change its paternalistic image in an effort to attract more college graduates with management potential.

The existing evidence also suggests that, other things being equal, increasing the amount of rewards that people derive from their jobs increases their job satisfaction and decreases the probability that they will voluntarily resign. Thus, other things being equal, an increase in a person's pay will make him more satisfied with his pay, an increase in his chances for promotion will make him more satisfied with his promotional opportunities. While this relationship seems to hold within any given person for any given dimension of reward, it should not be concluded that one can predict the level of a person's satisfaction from knowing the amount of reward he receives. For example, in one study it was observed that first-level supervisors making more than \$12,000 a year were substantially more satisfied with their pay than were company presidents making less than \$49,000. The explanation of this apparent anomaly brings to light an important psychological principle. A person compares his level of reward with that received by others who in his judgment are of comparable rank, merit, or worth. Information about what others receive provides the basis for the establishment of what is, to him, a fair or equitable level and he becomes satisfied when his level of reward reaches or exceeds the fair or equitable level. Thus, dissatisfaction is a matter of relative rather than absolute deprivation. Two people might be receiving exactly the same level of compensation but one might be highly satisfied and the other dissatisfied because they are comparing their salary level to different sets of persons or groups. Furthermore, an increase in compensation for one person may actually increase, rather than decrease, his dissatisfaction with his pay if it was accompanied by a larger increase to someone who he believed to be of comparable worth.

There is a related question which has received some attention, pertaining to the effects of secrecy concerning salary schedules. Some organizations, including state and local governments, have publicized salary schedules which permit the free flow of information about salaries within the organization. Others, and these are probably in the majority, encourage secrecy with respect to level of compensation. The assumption is that such a practice will prevent comparisons and mask what might be perceived and interpreted as inequities. While by no means definitive, a recent investigation by a psychologist at Yale University shows that secrecy does not prevent people from making wage comparisons but merely means that the comparisons will be based on imperfect and incomplete information. Managers, in the absence of reliable information about the compensation level of others, tend to overestimate the compensation of peers and of subordinates and to underestimate the compensation of superiors. Believing that one's peers and subordinates are receiving more compensation than, in fact, they were, was contributing to considerable dissatisfaction with their pay; and believing that one's superior was receiving less compensation than he was seriously reduced the promotional incentive.

PATERNALISTIC SYSTEM

The paternalistic system—which emphasizes providing people with large amounts of rewards primarily of an unconditional nature, undoubtedly has helped to attract and hold on to employees and, with the exception of the problems associated with perceived unfairness and inequity, has contributed to increased satisfaction on the part of employees. It is exceedingly doubtful, however, whether this system did anything 'significant by way of motivating employees while they were in the organization.

The distinction suggested is a distinction between a person's satisfaction with his job and with his company and his motivation to perform effectively in his job within that company. Once it was assumed that these two things went hand in hand, that a person who is satisfied with his job would necessarily be an effective performer within that job and, conversely, that a person who is dissatisfied with his job would necessarily be an ineffective performer. During the last 10 to 15 years, there have been approximately 50 research investigations conducted in order to test the correctness of this assumption. In each of these investigations, measurements were taken on the job satisfaction of individuals, typically through interviews or questionnaires, and these were correlated with measurements of the effectiveness of their performance. The obtained results indicate quite conclusively the inaccuracy of this assumption. There was no consistent or meaningful relationship between job satisfaction and job performance. Effective performers were as likely to be dissatisfied with their jobs as they were to be satisfied with their jobs, and ineffective performers were as likely to be satisfied with their jobs as they were to be dissatisfied.

A fairly consistent relationship has been observed between job satisfaction and turnover. The relationship is, as one might expect, a negative one. In other words, people who are satisfied with their jobs are much less likely to leave the organization than people who are dissatisfied with their jobs.

It is now fairly clear that the paternalistic approach was not a very effective strategy for dealing with the motivation problem. It operated primarily on job satisfaction and indirectly on people's decisions concerning whether to leave or stay in the organization and had relatively little, if any, effect on people's decisions about how much they would produce while in the organization. It was also in no sense a complete and integrated approach to management. While it is possible, and indeed necessary, for an organization to devote some of its resources to attracting future members to the organization and binding its members into the system, the paternalistic model was hardly a suitable guide for the decision-making process in organization. Clearly, there are other criteria for evaluating decisions than whether they will make the existing members of the organization happy.

SCIENTIFIC MANAGEMENT APPROACH

The second approach or strategy concerning how to motivate people within organizations is the scientific management approach. Like the paternalistic theory, this approach is also predicated on an assumption that people dislike work and that special conditions have to be created in organizations in order to induce them to work effectively. The scientific managment approach also makes extensive use of rewards. However, these rewards are conditional rather than unconditional. The rewards are attached to and made conditional upon effective performance. Each person is rewarded in accordance with his contribution to the system.

The scientific management approach represents an attempt to create, on the part of members or employees of organizations, something which is akin to the motivation of the independent entrepreneur. Such persons are in the position of receiving rewards in direct relationship to their accomplishment. If their business goes bankrupt, they lose their investment; if it prospers, they reap the benefits.

There are two related methods of simulating these conditions for members of organizations who do not share directly in the financial profits. One involves the establishment of standard rules, policies, or procedures and punishing those who deviate from them. Examples of this are warnings, reprimands, or even dismissals for violating rules or procedures. The other is to establish standards of good performance on each job and to reward people in accordance with the degree to which they meet these standards. The clearest example of the latter method may be found in individual wage incentives. Here the size of an individual's paycheck is presumably directly related to the amount of his performance. It is also manifest in such practices as promoting individuals on the basis of their merit and in recognizing and rewarding people for special accomplishments.

While there are some differences between the behavioral consequences of conditional punishments and of conditional rewards (for example, people are more likely to feel coerced, threatened, and antagonistic under a conditional punishment system), they tend to be used together in organizations and because the steps which must be taken to create these conditions are, in fact, quite similar.

If one is actually to set up a system based on these principles, at least three different steps have to be taken. First, one has to define the standards used in allocation of the rewards and punishments, i.e., to decide what behaviors are going to be rewarded and what behaviors are going to be punished. This involves a set of rather precisely defined rules and practices and an attempt on the part of the manager to specify in as exact terms as possible what he expects of each of his subordinates. Secondly, a system must be set up whereby the behavior of the subordinate is monitored or observed so that errors, misbehavior, or violation of rules, as well as superior performance can be observed and detected. Finally, in order to be effective, the system must actually allocate rewards or punishments on the basis of these observations of performance. Thus, in order to implement the principle of rewarding good performance and punishing poor performance, one must incorporate into the system centralized planning and control and close supervision.

In an organization founded on scientific management motivational principles, one would expect to find well-defined job descriptions. Each person would understand what is expected of him, i.e., the criteria on the basis of which he is to be evaluated. While there might be a job evaluation system, the range allocated to individual jobs or positions would be large, permitting considerable latitude for merit increases. Rates of promotion would be highly variable even for persons starting in the same positions. Some persons with objectively demonstrated merit would advance rapidly while others would advance more slowly if at all. The rate of dismissals or involuntary turnover would be high, particularly in comparison with the paternalistic system.

How would a manager behave in strict accordance with the scientific management approach? Quite clearly the burden would be on him to make, within his area of freedom and responsibility, decisions with respect to the behavior of his subordinates. He must communicate these policies and decisions as accurately and precisely as possible and check up on his subordinates to make sure that their actions are in accordance with them. Whenever an error is made or a violation of rules occurs, his reaction is to find out who is responsible and to mete out the appropriate disciplinary action as quickly as possible. Whenever a person exhibits behavior above and beyond the call of duty, he receives special commendation.

SCIENTIFIC MANAGEMENT

Unlike the paternalistic approach, which has little foundation in psychological research or theory, the scientific management approach is predicated on a strong psychological foundation. The foundation in this case is what psychologists have termed the law of effect or principle of reinforcement. Succinctly, it states that if a person undertakes an action, and this action is rewarded, that behavior or action will tend to be repeated. On the other hand, if the person undertakes an action which is followed by punishment, that behavior will tend not to be repeated. Research has provided support for this proposition in a large number of different situations and many of the techniques for controlling behavior outside of industry rest on the same foundations. It is also consistent with dramatic increases in performance obtained from the installation of wage incentives in some situations and with evidence from studies of managers and hourly workers showing that effective performers are more likely than ineffective performers to view performance on their present job as a means to the attainment of wage increases and a promotion to a higher level job.

The motivational basis of scientific management consists of external or organizational control over the worker while he is performing his job. When this system is functioning optimally, the individual does his job well not because he gets any particular satisfaction from so doing, but because he is compelled to do so by his environment. Effective performance is necessary in order to get the things he desires or avoid the things he fears.

It is clear that the techniques associated with the scientific management approach have been useful in many instances in industrial organization. I assume that life insurance companies, for example, have benefited greatly from the fact that their salesmen work on an incentive basis. Wage incentives have also demonstrated their usefulness in many production jobs and it is clear to me that our large universities have increased the research output of their faculty by the introduction of a publish-or-perish philosophy.

On the other hand, the scientific management approach does not appear to be universally applicable. Wage incentives, for example, require some basis for measuring performance and for communicating the standards to be used in measurement to those who are affected. This is quite clearly difficult for many jobs, particularly those of a staff or managerial nature.

If one considers only those situations in which performance can be measured, I believe it true that the conditional reward-punishment strategy is of greatest value when individuals have control over the outcomes on the basis of which the rewards and punishments are allocated. By control, I mean that the individuals can produce or not produce the outcomes at will. It would make little sense to reward individuals on sunny days and punish them on rainy days even if good weather were indispensable to the success of the operation. Similarly, it makes little sense from a motivational standpoint, to pay a person who works on a mechanized conveyer belt in accordance with the speed with which he works, or to reward a company director who has no control over the company profits, with a stock option plan.

Somewhat less obvious are instances of partial control. These are situations in which the individual can not completely determine the outcomes which are linked to rewards or punishments. There are two primary sources of partial control in organizations. One source lies in the nature of the task or job performed by the individual. In some tasks or jobs there is less than a one-to-one relationship between the behavior of the incumbent and the effectiveness of the incumbent and the effectiveness of his performance. Other events not under his control also affect how well he does. The physician may perform a perfect operation but the patient may die; the salesman may make an effective presentation but fail to get the sale, and the manager may do an unusually effective job of administering his division but fail to make a profit due to adverse market conditions. Other "chance" factors influence the level of performance and, to the degree to which this occurs, the conditional reward-punishment strategy fails to achieve its intended purpose. Success or failure is a matter of luck rather than skill or conscientious application of effort.

A similar result occurs as a consequence of the fact that a set of jobs are interdependent rather than independent. The performance of worker A is dependent on the performance of worker B, which in turn is dependent on the performance of worker C, and so on. In such instances, and they are quite common, it is difficult or impossible to trace errors or superior performance to the efforts of one individual. It is only the group or team effort which can be adequately evaluated and each person has but partial control over the team outcome.

There is clearly much more evidence for the scientific management approach to motivation than was the case for the paternalistic approach. However, it would seem to be more useful in some situations than in others. Specifically, the conditional reward-punishment system is most applicable to the degree to which (1) the assessment of the outcomes of individual performance is feasible, (2) the basis for the reward system is comprehensive and is made clear to the person, and (3) the attainment of the outcomes on the basis on which the rewards and punishments are allocated is under the individual's control. Under these three conditions, the scientific management system can and has played an important part in motivating individuals to high productivity.

PARTICIPATIVE MANAGEMENT THEORY

A third strategy for motivation is the participative management approach. This strategy is more recent than the other two but appears to have had, during its relatively short existence, an important influence on managerial practice.

Whereas paternalistic management assumed that man can be induced to work out of a feeling of gratitude to the system and scientific management assumed that man can be induced to work by the expectation of gain for so doing or the expectation of loss for not doing, participative management assumes that conditions can be created such that people derive satisfaction from doing an effective job per se. They can become ego involved in their jobs—emotionally committed to doing them well and taking pride from evidence that they are effective in furthering the goals of the company.

Little mention is made in these ideas of either compensation or promotion. The incentives for effective performance in the participative management approach are in the task or job itself, not in the consequences of task performance. In other words, it seeks to create conditions under which effective performance can be the goal, not the means to the attainment of the goal. It is based on self-control rather than organizational control.

There is in this proposal a great deal of contact and interaction between supervisor and subordinate, but it takes a form different from more traditional conceptions of management. Instead of telling a subordinate exactly what is to be done and how he is to do it, checking up on him to make sure that instructions have been carried out, and rewarding or punishing him depending on an assessment of his performance, this system entails working with the subordinate in defining and structuring his job responsibilities, and problem solving with him in a joint manner about difficulties or problems which he is experiencing in doing his job.

There is much more reliance in the participative management approach on the group as a problem-solving and decision-making unit. On matters affecting the entire unit, the supervisor does not make decisions autocratically and issue orders for subordinates but rather meets with the subordinates as a group, sharing problems with them and encouraging them to participate with him in finding solutions to these problems. Thus, the president of an organization can meet with his vice presidents as a group and they can work on problems ordinarily handled by the president alone or by the president meeting individually with his vice presidents. In turn, each vice president meets with his department heads, department heads meet with their division heads, and so on down the rank-and-file work group.

In effect, this entails participation by subordinates in the decision-making process which is assumed, with considerable justification, to create ego involvement on the part of subordinates in the decisions and identification with corporate goals.

This participative management approach to motivation is quite consistent with existing research results. A tremendous amount of research has been conducted within the last 10 to 15 years into the sources of differences between managers of high-productivity and low-productivity units. While there are some exceptions, the results generally support the notion that the managers of highly productive units are acting in accordance with the third strategy. This does not mean that this approach is equally effective under all conditions. In fact, it has been much more influential at higher than at lower organizational levels. One is more likely to find managers acting in accordance with the participative management strategy at upper and middle levels of management than on the shop floor.

Even at higher organizational levels I do not believe that we can afford to overlook the effects of compensation and promotion. Is a person who is highly ego involved in his job and identified strongly with corporate goals going to continue to produce at the same high level even though circumstances convince him that he is being greatly undercompensated relative to his peers? Even though he learns that his chances of promotion to a higher level position are nonexistent?

This raises the interesting possibility of an amalgam of the scientific management and participative management approaches.

There is no inconsistency between the notion of setting up conditions in organizations such that people are rewarded through wage increases and promotions for effective performance at the same time as they derive pleasure or satisfaction from observing that they have executed their responsibilities well. We can envision a system in which individuals are challenged by their jobs and are rewarded by the organization for doing them well.

An effective integration of the two sets of proposals would entail giving people as much freedom in planning their jobs as is consistent with the existing technology and tailoring the amount of rewards they receive with how effective they are. Evaluations of performance and hence compensation levels and promotional possibilities are based on results, not on adherence to arbitrary rules or supervisory whims and fancies.

Motivation and Merit:
Pay and Promotion

Edward E. Lawler, III

The best employee on a given job typically produces at least two times as much as the worst employee doing the job. In some instances the most effective employee's production is many times greater than that of the least effective employee. What accounts for this difference? Ability? Motivation? Certainly ability is a factor: yet employees equal in ability can have large differences in production because of motivational differences. What causes these motivational differences that seem to be so mysterious and difficult to understand? The answer—a large number of things, many of which are within the control of a manager and some which are not.

Childhood experiences, off the job activities and strength of motive all influence motivation, but they are beyond the control of the manager or the company. The manager is far from powerless, however. He does have control over two of the most important influences on employee motivation: the giving and withholding of rewards like pay and promotion and the design of the employee's job. By properly rewarding people and designing jobs, a manager can create conditions that will lead to a generally high level of motivation among subordinates.

In an earlier article (see *Vectors* 68/3) the influences of job design on motivation were discussed in detail. Briefly stated, motivational job design demands that people work on a whole product, receive feedback about their performances, have a voice in structuring their work and feel challenged by their job.

REWARDS

Probably the two most important rewards that any organization can give are money and promotion. Research evidence shows that the manner in which they

Reprinted from *ASTME/Vectors*, Vol. 4, No. 5 (September-October 1969) by permission of the author and the American Society of Tool and Manufacturing Engineers.

are given has a very definite impact on the motivation level present in the organization. An example is seen in a recent research project's findings on the handling of money and promotion in a sample of over one hundred R and D laboratories.

The directors of many of these labs said, "A promotion ladder exists upon which researchers can be promoted without their moving into management, and promotion on this ladder depends upon merit."'

Many researchers were not aware that technical promotion ladders were even operating in their organizations; most of those who were aware that such ladders were operating felt that promotion on them was not based upon performance.

The directors said, "Performance appraisals are regularly held and pay is based upon performance."

The researchers said that performance appraisals are not held regularly in their organization and that they are not at all sure that pay is based upon performance.

Clearly these directors and researchers had different views of the situation existing in their labs. Is this type of disagreement limited to superior-subordinate relationships in these particular labs? Definitely not. These kinds of differences have been found in all kinds of organizations. Whether the researchers' or the directors' description of the situation best fits reality really isn't important as far as motivation is concerned. The critical point is that the researchers' motivations are based on their perceptions of the situation and these perceptions are not motivating ones.

MOTIVATION THEORY

Motivation theory provides a clear guide as to the kind of perceptions that must exist if rewards like pay and promotion are to be motivators in an organization. According to the theory, rewards must be perceived to be important and obtainable as a result of good job performance. In the case of pay, this means that pay is a motivator of performance to the extent that it is *perceived* as being important, and to the extent that it is seen to be a result of good job performance. If either one of these conditions does not exist, pay cannot be a motivator. In the research and development labs studied, the problem was that pay was not perceived as related to performance. No matter how important pay is, it cannot be a motivator unless it is seen as dependent upon performance. Motivation theory also stresses the need to consider all the consequences of good performance in order to understand the degree to which a person will be motivated to carry it out. Thus, if important negative consequences also seem to result from good performance, an employee will not be motivated to perform well even though pay is important and tied to performance on the job.

Data collected from thousands of employees shows, as predicted by motivation theory, that the most motivated employees report that pay is important to them and that it is related to their performance. Thus, it would seem that all an organization need do to motivate its employees is (1) offer valued rewards, and (2) be sure that every employee believes that the receipt of these rewards is based upon his performance. However, this is a deceptively simple statement of the problem in one important respect. It glosses over the many difficult issues that arise when attempts are made to design actual rewards systems which will create these conditions. Let us consider the kinds of practices that must be put into force.

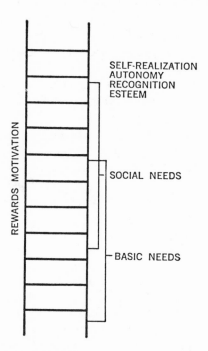

IMPORTANCE OF REWARDS

Motivation theory states that man can be thought of as possessing a number of needs and that these needs can be arranged in hierarchical form. At the bottom of the hierarchy are the basic survival needs for physiological well-being and security. In the middle of the hierarchy are the social needs, or the needs for meaningful associations with one's fellow man. Near the top of the hierarchy are the needs for esteem, recognition and autonomy, while at the very top is the need for self-realization, or full development of one's competence. The reason that it is important to think of these needs as being in a hierarchy is that, as the lower level needs are satisfied, they diminish in importance while the higher order needs grow in importance. This trend continues until the highest order need is activated. There is some evidence to suggest that the higher order needs are insatiable—that the nature of man is such that he can never be satisfied, no matter how much he obtains or accomplishes.

How does this thinking relate to the importance of the major rewards that an organization can give? None of the rewards an organization can give are listed as needs in the scheme. The thinking is relevant to the rewards because pay or promotion may satisfy some of the needs of people although they cannot satisfy every need.

People seek objects in their environment that they believe are relevant to the satisfaction of their needs. Thus, objects in the environment are important or attractive to people to the degree that they satisfy needs that are currently active within the person. They key question concerning the importance of a reward is—what needs can it satisfy?

In our society, pay can clearly satisfy security needs and the basic physiological needs for food and water. These needs are satisfied in most members of our society rather easily and by small amounts of money, but once they are satisfied they lose importance. As a consequence, pay can lose its ability to motivate.

Therefore, it seems clear that if pay is to remain important to most members of an organization, it must be seen as satisfying at least some of their higher order needs. The logical higher order needs that employees might see pay as satisfying are those of esteem and recognition.

For better or worse, modern society considers a person's pay a mark of his success and, therefore, an indicator of his status. If wages are the means by which these needs can be satisfied, they should remain important to a person despite the fact that he is earning a considerable amount of money and despite the fact that his lower order needs are satisfied. A good example of this is the case of the new company president who insisted that he receive a $200,000 salary rather than $100,000 salary plus deferred income. Because of taxes he would have netted more from the $100,000 offer, but he preferred straight salary because he wanted an impressive salary figure to show in the annual proxy statement. Promotions and status symbols like pay do satisfy esteem and recognition needs, and, because of this, they are important rewards to the individual.

Can organizations influence the degree to which rewards like pay are seen to satisfy esteem and recognition needs? The answer seems to be that they can have some influence, but their degree of influence is limited because what satisfies these needs is partially determined by society as a whole. Because of this, the motivation of an employee can never be completely controlled by the organization. In the case of modern society, high pay and high level jobs are generally seen as marks of distinction and some prestige is automatically ascribed to those who receive them. However, organization reward policies do have some influence in determining the degree to which an individual's salary or position will be taken as a mark of his accomplishment and status both by himself and others. Reward policies are important because they influence the degree to which high pay and position are perceived by the employees and others familiar with the company as being marks of accomplishment, versus being the result of luck, seniority, playing politics or other nonmerit factors.

It is important to remember that it is not high pay or position as such, but what they are assumed to represent that leads to a bestowal of high status on the person who receives them. They are simply symbolic ways of recognizing accomplishment. Thus, where pay and position are generally known not to represent accomplishment they lose the ability to satisfy needs like esteem and recognition. We have all wondered or asked after meeting a wealthy individual whether he earned or inherited his money. The implication of this question (in terms of what his money means to us) is clear. Similarly, in organizations where pay and promotion are not merit based, salary and position may not be important determinants of status. In these cases, the amount of an employee's pay may become less important to him because he no longer sees it as a way of satisfying his esteem and recognition needs. In short, the first way organizations can guarantee that the rewards of pay and promotion will be important to employees is to create the belief that they are based upon merit, so that they will be looked to as an indication of accomplishment. However, the job of convincing people that rewards are based upon performance is far from simple and certainly not easy.

PUBLIC RECOGNITION

A second suggestion which can assure that rewards remain important is implicit in the statement by the company president cited previously; the amount of his pay was important to him because it was public knowledge. The fact that it was public made it that much more relevant as a vehicle for satisfying inherently public needs like esteem and recognition. Similarly, promotion is an important reward because it is visible and therefore effective in satisfying needs for recognition and esteem. High pay can only satisfy these needs if salaries are known. In most companies, managers' salaries are carefully guarded secrets and, as a result, it is not immediately obvious who the higher paid managers are in those companies.

Salary level can, of course, be estimated from the manager's job in the company and from how and where he lives. Undoubtedly a large part of the pattern of conspicuous consumption referred to as "keeping up with the Joneses" comes about because people want to show that they are as highly paid and successful in their jobs as the next person. The prestige that results from conspicuous consumption is presumably derived from the fact that it reflects salary size which in turn reflects the value an organization places on the individual's contribution. At best, this is an imperfect way of revealing the organization's regard for the individual, for small differences in pay are not noticeable and often even large differences are not immediately apparent.

Because of secrecy, differences in pay levels and amounts of absolute salary are often less important to managers than they would be if salary structures were public knowledge. A poor salary can be hidden from others—it isn't always obvious who receives the good salary. Salary is a relative matter and it is only when the salary structure is known that one can make accurate comparisons for the purpose of deciding what salary means in terms of esteem by the organization. Making this information public sensitizes people much more to small differences in salaries and can undoubtedly cause them to be more concerned about the relative size of their salaries, because their prestige rises or falls with a high or low public salary. This, of course, only happens where merit is considered the basis of pay, in which case actual salary differences exist for people holding similar jobs.

So far the focus has been on the possibility of organizations influencing the value of rewards like pay and promotion so that they can be effective motivators. As has been stressed, organization control is limited in this area since the value of rewards like pay and promotion are determined by many factors that are beyond the control of the organization. Organizations do have control over which rewards they offer, however, and this can be used to advantage in motivating employees. Because of the many factors that influence the value of rewards, large individual differences arise in how much employees value rewards like pay and promotion. The perceptive manager recognizes these differences and capitalizes on them by motivating his subordinates with the rewards they value. This may mean that he stresses pay for one subordinate, promotion for another and a status symbol for another. This is often a more productive approach than trying to get everyone to respond to pay by trying to make it important to everyone.

REWARDS TIED TO PERFORMANCE

If company-given rewards are to be motivators, employees must see them as being tied to performance. Organizations have relatively little control over whether rewards are important to people; but they have a great deal of control over the belief that rewards are tied to performance. Here the organization's policies are paramount in importance, for these policies can create this belief. For illustrative purposes the focus of this discussion will be on pay, but the points made are valid for other rewards.

Large differences must exist between the pay raises given to the good and poor performers. It is not enough to give the good performers a 10 percent annual raise and the poor performers a 3 percent raise. This is hardly a discriminable amount when salaries are secret, therefore differences this small may not seem worth working for. Ideally, each person's pay should be divided into three components with one component based strictly on the job the employee is doing. All employees holding similar jobs would receive the same amount for this component. A second part of the pay package should be determined by seniority and cost of living factors. Again, everyone in the company should receive this through automatic adjustment on an annual basis. The third part of the package, however, should not be automatic—it should be individualized according to performance in the preceding period. The poorest performer in the organization would receive nothing for this part of his pay package. However, the best performer would find that this part of his pay package would be as great as the other two parts combined. This would not be a raise, however, since it would vary from year to year with performance. The purpose of this kind of system is, of course, to make a large proportion of an individual's pay depend upon his performance during the current period. Thus, performance is chronologically tied closely to large changes in pay.

Contrast this for a moment with the system used in R and D labs mentioned earlier, and, in many other organizations. Small raises are usually given to most employees annually with the best performer getting perhaps a 7 percent greater raise than the worst performer and no one getting a pay cut: an individual can coast for a year and—assuming he has received good raises in the past—still be highly paid. On the other hand, an individual can improve greatly in performance in one year, but require several years to catch up with others in similar jobs if he has previously received raises which were smaller.

In traditional systems pay rates do not reflect current or recent performance levels although they may, to some extent, reflect total performance during an individual's stay in an organization. This serves to create the perception that pay is not based upon performance. Similar problems develop in promotion systems—some people are promoted for reasons of seniority, others for performance, and others for convenience. Thus the connection between promotion and performance is destroyed and promotion ceases to be a motivator. If, on occasion, organizations promote on the basis of nonperformance factors they should clearly state this, but they should also state that a certain number of promotions will be determined on the basis of performance.

PERFORMANCE APPRAISALS

The really difficult problem in any reward system is that of measuring performance—an underlying fault of the R and D labs example mentioned earlier. In these organizations there existed a phenomenon that can be called the *vanishing performance appraisal.* Because the superiors were so indirect and nonconfronting in what they considered the appraisal session, the subordinates did not realize that their performance was being appraised.

A measure of performance must meet several requirements. It must be a valid measure of performance from the point of view of top managment. And it must lead to promotion and pay decisions that are acceptable to people throughout the entire organization. This means supervisors, subordinates and peers must all accept the results of the system. It is crucial that this wide acceptance be obtained because without it, rewards will not generally be seen to reflect merit. Employees gain much of their knowledge about how rewards are given by watching what happens to other people in the organization. If they feel that those doing good work are rewarded, they accept the existence of a merit reward system. On the other hand, if people they don't respect receive raises, the belief in a merit pay system breaks down. Obviously, the more the appraisal system yields decisions congruent with the consensus about employees' performance, the greater the likelihood that employees will believe that a merit system does exist. The performance measure that is used should also be such that employees feel their contributions to the organization show up in it very directly. They must feel they have control over it; for that to happen it should not reflect things other than their own performances, so that what they do has little weight.

The performance appraisal systems that are actually used by organizations run all the way from superiors making subjective judgments on various traits to the complicated "objective" accounting-based systems that are used to measure managers' effectiveness. The problem with the subjective judgments of a superior is obvious: the subordinates often see them as arbitrary decisions based upon inadequate information—and simply unfair. The objective systems are perhaps the fairest in many ways, but they often fail to reflect individual efforts. Stock option plans are an example. With such plans, pay is tied to the price of the stock on the market. This, presumably, motivates employees to work hard so that the price of the stock will go up. The problem with this approach is, of course, that most managers see the connection between their efforts and the price of the stock as being very weak. Similarly, plans that base bonuses on profit centers or on the effectiveness of certain parts of the business can work, but all too often the profitability of the organization is controlled more by outside forces than by inside efforts.

Another problem with objective systems is illustrated by the results of most piece-rate incentive plans used at the worker level. These plans are based on the illusion that objective, highly measurable rates can be scientifically set, and, that trust between superiors and subordinates is not necessary for the sytem to work since it is, after all, "objective." Years of experience with these systems show that effective piece-rate systems simply cannot be established where foremen and workers do not trust each other and do not have a participative relationship. No completely objective system has ever been designed, nor will one ever be. Unexpected contingencies will always arise which have to be worked out between superiors and subordinates, and they can only be resolved in a way that does not destroy the reward system where mutual trust exists between superiors and subordinates. When poor relationships exist, workers strive to get rates set high and then restrict their production because they simply don't believe good performance will, in fact, lead to higher pay in the long run.

The answer seems to rest in a reasonable combination of subjective superior-based rating systems and systems which use more objective measures. In developing such a system we must accept the fact that the system can never be 100 percent objective and that subjective judgments will always be important. Further, we must realize that the key to broad acceptance of the decisions yielded by the appraisal system depends upon the broadest possible participation within the organization.

THE SYSTEM

What would such a system look like? It would necessarily be based upon superior-subordinate appraisal sessions where subordinates feel that they have a genuine opportunity to influence the boss. Obviously such a system cannot operate—nor can any other for that matter—unless good superior-subordinate relations exist so that mutual influence is possible. In the first appraisal session the superior and subordinate should jointly decide on three things. First, they should decide on the objectives the subordinate should try to achieve during an ensuing time period. This period might last from three months to several years depending on the level of the job. Second, they should decide on the manner in which the subordinate's progress toward these objectives can be measured. Here, of course, objective measures might be used as well as subjective ratings by peers and others. Third, they should decide on the level of reward the subordinate will receive if he accomplishes his objective. A second meeting should be held at the end of the specified time period in order that the superior and the subordinate can jointly assess the progress of the subordinate and decide upon any pay actions. Finally, a few weeks later the whole process should begin again with another objectives-setting session. The advantages of this kind of system extend far beyond reward administration. It can create a situation where superiors and subordinates jointly recognize more clearly the subordinate's actual job duties and responsibilities. It also offers the subordinate a chance to become involved in important decisions about his own future and thereby encourages a kind of give and take that seldom exists between superiors and subordinates.

With this kind of performance evaluation program a good connection should be created between rewards and performance. On the other hand, if salary secrecy is maintained, the positive connection may not be as apparent to everyone as it should be. One of the findings that has consistently appeared in the author's research on pay is that managers tend to have incorrect information about the pay of the other managers in the organization. Specifically, they have a general tendency to overestimate the pay of the managers around them. For example, in one organization the average raise given was 6 percent, yet the managers believed that it was 8 percent. The larger their own raise was, the larger they believed other people's raises to be. This resulted in the wiping out of many of the effects of the differential reward system that were actually operating in the company. Regardless of how well the individual manager performed, he was faced with a situation where he felt he was getting less than an average raise. This problem was particularly severe among the high performers. Although they believed they were performing well, they received what appeared to them to be less than average raises, which did nothing to encourage them to believe that pay was based upon merit. This was especially ironic since their pay *did* in fact reflect their performance on the job.

Making pay information more public will not in itself establish the belief that pay is based upon merit. All it can do is clarify those situations where pay actually is based upon merit but where it is not obvious because relative salaries are not accurately known. The crucial factor in making pay a motivator is, of course, the effective tying of pay to performance, which must happen first. Making pay rates public where pay is not tied to performance will only emphasize even more dramatically that pay is not tied to performance, thereby making pay even less of a motivator.

REWARDS AS MOTIVATORS?

The answer to the question of whether an organization should try to motivate its employees by using rewards like pay and promotion depends partially upon whether the organization is in a situation where it can move to such things as openness and participative performance appraisals. One of the most striking ironies concerning the use of pay as a motivator becomes obvious when this issue is considered. It is the organizations that most need to use pay as a motivator that are the least likely to be successful in using it for that purpose. The autocratically-run organization which depends heavily upon rewards like pay and promotion and upon punishments like dismissal in order to motivate employees is in no position to build the employee relationships that will allow a creditable reward system to be established within its structure.

A successful reward system is not made up solely of a set of policies; it must have these, but it also must be based upon a high degree of trust between superiors and subordinates. In the traditional autocratic organization it would be impossible for superiors and subordinates to have the kinds of goal-setting sessions that must take place if the results of the appraisal system are going to be accepted. This kind of organization can, and frequently does, have widely differing pay rates supposedly tied to performance, but, because these rates are set from above, it is difficult for the employees to accept them as being merit-based. In addition, an autocratically-run organization is not likely to be able to tolerate openness about rewards like pay. Openness is effective only if existing pay differentials can be justified by management. The whole idea of justifying pay differentials to subordinates is foreign to the traditional approach to management. What has happened in most organizations where salary secrecy exists and where salaries have not had to be generally justified is that, because of conveniences of the moment, the salary systems have ceased to be justifiable. When this is true, openness about salaries is bound to cause problems, although this can be good if it forces a cleanup of the system.

The situation should be quite different in an organization which subscribes to what has been called modern organization theory. Since this type of management emphasizes participation and self-control, the motivational reward system described can flourish. Openness about salary is natural in this kind of organization and the type of performance appraisal system described is consonant with the idea of self-control. This view of management, in essence, argues that people can provide useful inputs to the evaluative process, and, that they are willing to accept rewards based upon their performance. It is ironic that pay and other rewards can be effective motivators in this kind of organization because much of the argument for creating this type of organization has rested upon the belief that employees can be effectively motivated by nonfinancial motivators. This style of management often claims that it leads its employees who are more involved in their jobs and who have greater job-related opportunities to satisfy higher order needs. Thus, in some ways it is less important that pay be used as a motivator because of the other motivators present when this style of management is used.

There are some other factors that should be kept in mind when consideration is given to using rewards to motivate employees. Sometimes it just isn't possible to develop a measure of individual performance that will be seen as valid by the individual, his peers and his managers. When this is the case, the attempt to use rewards to motivate employees may cause more problems than it will solve. Under these conditions it is impossible to clearly relate rewards to performance, and, thus, the giving of rewards differentially to employees will only cause bitterness and mistrust. In some situations, although individual performance is not measurable, group performance may be, and in these instances it sometimes makes sense to relate the giving of rewards to group performance. It also makes sense to use group performance as a basis for rewarding employees when a great deal of cooperative behavior is needed to get work done. Group reward plans motivate cooperative behavior while individual incentive plans often discourage it since cooperative behavior is not explicitly rewarded.

One of the advantages of pay as a motivator is that it can be given on a group basis or an individual basis and it can be given in widely different amounts. Unfortunately, promotion is not so flexible a reward. Promotion can only be given on an individual basis. And it can be given only when old positions are open or new ones created, although it can be held out as an incentive at all times. Thus, an organization that relies on promotion as its major reward can get into difficulty because of its low flexibility. This argues for the use of pay as the most practical reward in organizations that decide to motivate their employees through the use of extrinsic rewards.

SUMMARY

It seems that organizations should try to use extrinsic rewards as motivators if they are at a stage in their development where (1) meaningful participative performance appraisals sessions can take place between superiors and subordinates (2) information can be made public about how the rewards are given (3) superiors are willing to explain and support the reward system in discussions with their subordinates (4) rewards can be varied widely depending upon the individual's current performance (5) performance can be measured. On the other hand, if these things cannot be done, perhaps it is better not to count on using extrinsic rewards as motivators. Just adopting some of the practices mentioned that are necessary if rewards are to be really effective motivators (*e.g.*, openness), or putting them all into an organization where the conditions are not right (*e.g.*, where good superior-subordinate relations do not exist) may only make the situation worse.

Motivating Men
With Money

Saul W. Gellerman

Nearly everyone "knows" why money affects the motivation of workers: that is, they know the standard folklore about money which has endured, largely unquestioned, since the dawn of the industrial revolution. By this reckoning, money is supposed to be the main reason, if not the only one, that most people have for working at all. Knowing how to motivate is supposed to consist largely of knowing how to dangle money as artfully as possible before the eyes of one's subordinates.

The behavioral scientist, on the other hand, knows that folklore cannot be used as a guide by managers trying to motivate today's educated and mobile employee. At one time, fear of losing the chance to make any money at all may have been enough to make people work harder. But that is seldom true today. Income now operates chiefly as a price mechanism to distribute the labor supply among employers; it rarely affects job performance in any lasting or significant way. Most salary, bonus, and profit-sharing plans and many commission and incentive-pay plans do not motivate any action other than the purely passive one of staying in the organization.

To say that monetary omnipotence is a myth is not to say that money is impotent. Money can motivate; that is, it can influence action and encourage extra effort, extra creativity, or any other kind of non-routine performance. But it can do this only when the increment or net gain for the employee is large enough.

Let's begin by taking a closer look at what an increment is. Essentially, it is a change in pay having three characteristics. First, an increment can never be

Reprinted from *Fortune*, Vol. LXXVII, No. 3 (March, 1968) by permission of the publisher. The article was condensed from *Management By Motivation* published by The American Management Association, 1968.

described in an entirely objective way, even when its dollar-and-cent value is known precisely. Whatever symbolism money has for the individual and whatever presumptions or illusions he has about how added income would affect the way he lives are as much a part of the increment for him as is the money itself. Equivalent increments for two or more people are not necessarily equivalent at all interms of their actual effects. The importance of an increment is as much in the eye of the beholder as in its monetary value.

Second, an increment is relative. How an individual may be expected to react to an increase in salary depends on his existing income, his net worth, his history of income growth and capital ownership, and his own estimate of the marketability of his services. In general, the more a man has or is accustomed to having, the larger the increment must be to impress him.

Finally, an increment is always something extra, in the sense that it is added to income that is already guaranteed or expected. An increment that is large enough to motivate more than mere "membership" in the company must reach a certain critical size that is determined by the individual's estimate of the cost of a safe but radical change in his financial condition.

Any sizable change in an individual's financial condition, whether it results from a raise, a promotion, or a job with a new company, involves certain uncertainties, discomforts, and anxieties. The most common uncertainty about high income is whether it is sustainable. The most common discomforts are greater commitments of time and effort to maintaining the new financial position. The most common anxieties involve a change in role; that is, the necessity of loosening old social ties and forming new ones. All these intangible considerations represent what the individual thinks he may be asked to sacrifice in exchange for higher income. The more he values what he fears he may lose, or the less certain he is about what he may have to lose, the greater the cost of the increment will appear to be; and accordingly, the higher the increment must be to offset this cost. In fact, it is not sufficient merely to offset the psychological cost of agreeing to a sizable increment. There must be a clear, sizable net gain. Therefore, liberality is essential. An individual who is likely to be plagued by second thoughts about the wisdom of his commitments is not effectively motivated. This does not mean unrestricted access to the corporate treasury, but it does mean providing a margin for error in the individual's favor.

MOST PEOPLE HAVE A PRICE

It would be easy to argue that no monetary price can be set on intangibles such as uncertainty or anxiety. But that really depends on the individual's values. If he prizes something that money can buy, or if he values something that money can symbolize, a sufficiently liberal increment *can* offset his anxieties. In other words, some people, perhaps most people, do have a price, and there is nothing necessarily dishonorable or reprehensible about that. What is "sold" in these transactions is not necessarily honor; it is more likely to be the luxury of inaction and immunity from worry.

To be effective, the net gain must also be large enough to assure the individual of some degree of safety. Safety in this sense refers to protection against getting less than one had bargained for, either because of some unforeseen hazard or because the new arrangements somehow fail to work the way they were supposed to. Precisely because an increment has to be big to be effective, it is likely to encounter skepticism. Consequently, it has to include some form of "insurance," either in the way it is paid or in the traditions of the firm that offers it. The greater the apparent hazard in accepting the opportunity to earn the increment, the greater the increment has to be in order to motivate effectively.

Finally, the increment must bring about a radical change in the individual's financial condition. The change must be more than one of degree; that, after all, could be expected to occur eventually anyway, at less hazard and at lower cost. It must be a change in order of magnitude. It must make possible things only dreamed of ordinarily. Unless the increment is princely, it is unlikely to excite the imagination or whet the appitite. It must do more than just raise income; it must change the individual's capital position. It must enable the traditional debtor to get out from under his debts; it must enable the man of no means to acquire at least some degree of real wealth. In short, the increment in income must change the individual's basic attitude toward money. That obviously requires a lot of money. Make no mistake about it; effective motivation with money is no piker's game.

As we have pointed out, income motivates only membership, not productivity. Where most wage and salary programs run into difficulty is in failing to recognize that this is also true of expected increases in income. Raises are, in effect, continually chasing the moving target of employee expectations. It does not take a mathematician to project on the basis of past history approximately when increases will occur and how large they will be. It is rare for employees to be surprised by the timing or the size of their pay increases. They may be disappointed, but they are seldom surprised.

Consider the psychological effects of this predictability of increases in income. When the expected increase is still remote, the prospect of it serves to. motivate membership, provided that the increase is expected to be equitable. (One can avoid the unpleasant necessity of looking around for another job by maintaining the illusion that the expected increase will be satisfactory.) As the time comes nearer when the increase is expected, the main things it motivates are curiosity and alertness for confirming signs that it will indeed occur.

If the increase does not occur on schedule, that fact will generate disappointment, feelings that the system is unjust, and perhaps, if the delay is prolonged, a search for another job. Or the individual may be motivated to complain, not necessarily about money alone, but about all the petty annoyances he is ordinarily willing to tolerate. He may even feel compelled, as a matter of pride, to reduce his performance level to a point that is commensurate with his now "inadequate" income.

If a raise does occur on schedule but is less than the individual expected, he may very well feel that he has been deceived. It is easier to live with this feeling, after all, than to acknowledge that he has been unrealistic in his expectations. This sense of disillusionment will not necessarily lower future expectations. It is more likely to make the individual cynical about his company and mistrustful of what it attempts to tell him. On the other hand, if the increase is about equal to what the individual expected, the company will be seen as having purchased his continued membership at a fair price. The experience will reassure him that the system to which he is attached is fair and responsive. But these reassurances only satisfy; they do not motivate him to work harder.

A WORLD OF INGRATES

If the increase exceeds the employee's expectations, either of two reactions is possible. There is some evidence that when certain people feel they are overpaid, they will actually increase their output to a point that justifies their new earning level. Other people, however, are less interested in justifying their income than in protecting it. They are likely to develop various restrictive practices that have the effect of monopolizing their overpaid jobs. Both reactions have the same underlying psychology: this is too good to last, and therefore something must be done to keep it from being found out and changed.

With the exception of the first reaction to an underestimated increase, the motivational effects of expected increases are very small indeed. For all practical purposes, an expected increase in income is already the property of the individual. Psychologically, the raise is already incorporated into what he regards as his earnings base; it is not "something extra."

In fact, satisfaction from money results primarily from an *increase* in income, not from income itself. Most people are, in a sense, ingrates. They regard their current income level as something they have already earned, rather than as something to be especially savored or appreciated. Thus the fact that an employer may pay his employees quite well relative to the outside labor market will not, as a rule, make his employees feel particularly grateful. It may motivate them to stay, however, and that is often more important than gratitude. But it is the experience of an earnings increase that provides them with satisfaction—and perhaps even with some temporary feelings of gratitude as well. It is the anticipation of an increase that provides them with excitement and perhaps even with an incentive to help it happen through conspicuous effort or diligence. It is the lack of an increase, when one is expected, that causes dissatisfaction.

It is a stubborn and extremely important fact of life that expectations of an increase in earnings tend to recur periodically, almost regardless of income level, effort, or accomplishment. Pay increases interrupt the cycle, but only temporarily. Many people therefore spend more time being dissatisfied with their incomes than being satisfied with them. Even people who are relatively well paid, in terms of objective indexes, will spend a significant part of their careers in a state of relative dissatisfaction with their pay.

We can now begin to see that compression of corporate salary scales works against motivation and makes most compensation programs basically satisfiers or dissatisfiers, not motivators. When the monetary gap between pay levels is relatively small, it is not likely that any single increase will be sizable enough to motivate action before it is granted or to motivate "justifying performance" after it is granted.

INSURANCE FOR EXECUTIVE RISK

Compressed salary scales are especially undesirable when they reduce the organization's ability to provide higher management personnel with "insurance" for the risks they incur in accepting heavy responsibilities. Responsibility and exposure increase together. The greater a man's responsibilities, the less the organization can afford to tolerate ineffective work and the greater the possibility that he may have to be relieved, perhaps precipitately, of those responsibilities. To compensate a man for accepting these risks, the proportional dollar gaps between executive salary levels should be greater than the gaps between lower management pay levels. If the gaps at higher levels are not large enough, executives may ask themselves whether it might not be wiser to decline a promotion in order to preserve an already high income at an acceptable risk level. That is, they may decide that their ratio of income to personal cost is already at its maximum level and could only worsen if they accepted a modest increase in pay in exchange for a sizable increase in risk. If too many executives begin to regard promotion as a bad financial bargain, top jobs may go by default to imprudent risk takers—exactly the kind of men who should not be given high-level responsibilities.

Thus pay increments must be large enough to excite the imagination, or to change fundamental attitudes toward money, if they are to have any hope of motivating extraordinary performance. But effective increments are not economically feasible on a large scale. They cost too much. If they are to be used at all, they must be rationed; and this raises the ticklish question of exactly who should be singled out to receive them. Generally speaking, effective increments should be offered only to people who are susceptible to them; that is, people who are likely to respond, for whatever psychological reason, with the desired action. These also must be people who are capable of some singularly important contribution to the organization—something they would be unlikely to attempt unless they were unusually motivated. Both susceptibility and capacity must be present. Further, there is little point in paying a premium for performance that would probably be attempted even without extra pay. Consequently, it is a relatively rare type of task that lends itself to effective increments. The task must include risks, discomforts, or difficulties that would ordinarily preclude attempts to accomplish it. In short, the combination of men and jobs for which effective increments are appropriate is quite rare.

There are at least two groups of men who could be motivated by large increments. First, some men are capable of leading the way into "breakthrough" areas that change the whole mission or strategy of an organization. The classic example was Charles P. Steinmetz, whose inventions practically created an industry for General Electric. One does not have to reach the towering stature of a Steinmetz, however, to qualify for effective increments. Creative work in such fields as product development, organizational analysis, and investment or acquisition analysis could, in the right circumstances, qualify for the large-increment treatment. Doing jobs of these kinds properly sometimes demands courage—the consequences of a mistake can be so horrendous that the individual's reputation is at risk along with his security. But it is plainly in the organization's interest to have decisions of these kinds made solely on the basis of capable men's judgments, undiminished by any fears for their own future. Thus an increment large enough to overcome their natural tendency to play it safe could be more than amply repaid by the results. Whether this would or would not be a gamble for the organization depends entirely on the wisdom with which the man, the job, and the increment itself were selected.

THE HOTHOUSE TREATMENT

Large increments could also be used effectively to motivate men who are capable of developing their managerial abilities faster, and ultimately better, than others. Such a man requires, above all, exposure to heavy doses of responsibility—often before he really feels ready. Increments that are liberal enough to pave the way to a wholly new financial status could be an effective way of encouraging such people to accept the risks of moving ahead rapidly. The game, in other words, should be worth the candle. Some companies already recognize this principle by tying part of the compensation growth rate of selected young "high potential" men to an estimate of that potential rather than to their current job level.

It is worth noting at this point that heavy responsibility is not, in itself, a justification for large increments. Responsibility is continual and must therefore be paid for continually in the form of salary. This means in effect that top executives will not necessarily be the most logical recipients of large increments, despite the fact that they currently receive nearly all the increments that could be classified as effective in a motivational sense. Depending on the needs of the organization, effective increments may be used more appropriately with scientific or professional personnel, or even with junior levels of management, than with executives.

The most obvious objection to granting large increments is that they could destroy the incentive to work, since work would no longer be an economic necessity. But there is little evidence that the acquisition of wealth decreases the motivation to work. Wealth makes people more selective about the work that they do, but it seldom makes them less interested in occupying their time constructively. Meaningful work is not inherently distasteful to most men, at least not the kind of men who are likely to accomplish something worthy of being paid for by large increments.

Nevertheless, there can be some serious problems associated with the rapid growth of income. Some young men who have experienced a rapid rise in income become blasé about the prospect of further increases. This too-much-too-soon phenomenon is more complex than it may at first appear. For one thing, young men whose income has risen rapidly may have jobs that they have tolerated largely for the sake of money—jobs that they have regarded as a temporary and expedient means of rapidly arriving at a position of financial comfort. Once the job has fulfilled its purpose, it may no longer be so easy to tolerate.

These young men are not entirely disenchanted with money, even though they are sometimes willing to accept a modest financial sacrifice to switch to jobs more to their liking. The problem is that their base has grown so large that the prospect of an increment large enough to motivate them has become quite remote. Once this happens, the bloom can come off the monetary rose very quickly, and they become more responsive to nonfinancial motivators.

When income seems to exceed what a job is worth, the excess is of course welcome; but it does not motivate. That is, overpay does not necessarily lead to higher sustained output than equitable pay, *if* the job itself does not seem to deserve the extra pay. The job, not the money, is the limiting factor. And large increments make sense only when the individual can—and knows he can—deliberately make a substantial difference in the results of his work.

ENCOURAGING GENIUS

Arguments against the broader use of very large increments usually boil down to the notion that few people, if any at all, are really worth that much to their employers. In this view, effective increments are a colossal and unnecessary waste of the stockholders' or taxpayers' money. And that objection reveals the heart of the problem of money motivation.

We have argued that to use money effectively as a motivator, it must be used with discrimination, but on a princely scale. It must be used to make men wealthy. But there is considerable resistence to the idea of deliberately making certain men wealthy. This comes not merely from socialist and egalitarian trends in society as a whole but, more important, from certain biases common to management itself. The fact is that most of the great productivity increases in recent memory did not happen because individuals resolved to do more. Rather, they resulted from the introduction of new tools, new products, and new processes. These in turn reflect the coordinated efforts of very large groups of people, rather than a few individuals. This has focused management's attention upon managing large groups, which means keeping peace through equitability of wages and salaries and the consequent use of money as a buyer of membership.

In other words, the nonmotivational use of money traces back to the assumption that individual effort really doesn't count. That assumption is often true. There have been very few Steinmetzes, Ketterings, or Lands to put the G.E.'s, G.M.'s, or Polaroids on the map. The conclusion drawn from this experience is that genius must be an extremely scarce commodity. So most managers assume that they should not wait for a genius to show up, but should instead harness the efforts of ordinary men in the most practical ways available.

The logic in that strategy rests on the rather tenuous assumption that genius needs no encouragement, that it will somehow come storming through in spite of itself. But not all geniuses are self-motivated, obstacle-ignoring heroes, and that is precisely why most of the potential geniuses in this world remain only potential geniuses. Those few men who do accomplish exceptional things and are recognized as geniuses are considerably brighter than average men; but they are not necessarily more gifted than, say, the top 5 or 10 percent of the population, most of whom accomplish nothing really extraordinary in a lifetime. There is, in other words, an enormous reservoir of relatively untapped genius—that is, men with the capacity for exceptional accomplishment—which existing systems of motivation have failed to reach.

One reason why the potential contribution of individuals to their organizations is often underestimated is that it is seldom in the individual's best interests to be as productive as he could be. Most people function far below their capacity mainly because of the essentially dependent relationship of any individual to the organization that employs him. When a man is financially dependent upon the continuity of his paychecks, he will be more interested in preserving that continuity than in inflating the next check.

This is most familiarly and dramatically seen in the tendency of production workers to restrict their output, even in the face of incentive payments. Their usual rationale is that to exceed a certain level of production would invite management to increase their quotas, or that it would create intolerably divisive strains between the more efficient and the less efficient workers, or that management would profit so disproportionately that it would be tantamount to letting themselves be used for someone else's advantage.

Something quite comparable occurs at higher organizational levels. It is equally against the interests of the executive to rock the boat by disagreeing with the opinions of his peers or superiors, or to take risks whose payoff is uncertain, or to make decisions that could be difficult to explain. Thus the executive's productivity may be limited by his own concern for security and the continuity of his income.

CREDIBLE EXECUTIVES

The basic problem in elevating performance levels is somehow to eliminate dependency, or at least to reduce it. But dependency, in the last analysis, is subjective; there is no way to measure "real" dependency or to say that one man's situation makes him more or less dependent than another man. A man is as dependent as he feels and acts. Thus the problem narrows to finding those people who would *feel* independent if they were given suitable financial treatment. We have to find people who are already predisposed to act independently and provide sufficient financial support to help them step over the line.

It is very much in an organization's interest to place its fortunes in the hands of men whose fortunes are *not* tied to the organization's, men who work because they want to work rather than because they have to. This is not merely for the sake of risk taking and nonconformity. If there is any single quality that is required of a man at higher management levels it is *credibility:* the ability to make unpopular or unwelcome points without being suspected of masking the truth for some ulterior motive. A credible executive can protest, for example, that a production target is impossible, without being suspected of merely bargaining for an easier goal. He can warn his superiors as dramatically or, if need be, as annoyingly as they must be warned in order to convince them that a projected action is dangerous, without fearing that he will lose their esteem. A credible executive is one whose inputs to the management decision process are listened to, not discounted; and for that reason his impact on the fortunes of his firm is much greater than that of dozens of peers who are, if you will, "incredible."

There are many ways to become credible, and undoubtedly the best of these is through demonstrated good judgment and ability. But when a man has done that, he is still not necessarily free of the consequences of his dependency. This is a subtle but extremely important point; even if an executive is in fact undeterred by his dependency, he is not freed of the suspicion of being deterred. He will find himself bargained with and fenced with in an endless attempt to estimate the "truth" behind his words, in spite of the fact that he may be concealing nothing. To be credible, a man must have more than just ability. His motives must be unquestioned. He must have nothing to gain or lose except his pride; and it must be apparent to those who deal with him that the desire to be proved right, not gain or safety, is his real motive. Thus credibility can hinge, in the last analysis, on independence, and *credible* independence hinges on wealth.

THE "IMPACT" FACTOR

Money can therefore motivate exceptional accomplishments in two ways: (1) through the prospect of becoming wealthy—that is, of a radical improvement in one's financial circumstances, and (2) by becoming irrelevant, by freeing the individual of both real dependency and the tendency of others to suspect him of the tactics of dependency. But if men are to be made wealthy deliberately in order to increase their effectiveness, it must be done selectively, not indiscriminately.

It is vitally important that measurements be found to determine whether the treatment is deserved. Not only must an extraordinary investment be carefully audited, but a convincing demonstration of the equitability of the investment must also be available. Otherwise, the effects of this treatment upon those who do not receive it could be costly and troublesome enough to cancel out whatever benefits the recepient produces. But in those exceptional jobs for which specific, critical, and exceptionally important actions can be isolated—actions that set the individual's achievement apart from all others and radically affect the fortunes of the organization as a whole—large increments are probably the best guarantee that the action will be taken effectively.

This leads to another important point about the use of effective increments; namely, the kind of organization that can use them. If the decision to pay an individual large increments or not is based in part on the magnitude of the impact that his actions can have on the organization, it follows that effective increments are appropriate only in an organization that wants to be heavily impacted—that wants, in other words, to change. Effective increments are incompatible with maintaining the status quo. But they are very well suited to the needs of an organization that wants deliberately to change its products, markets, size, or profitability.

ADDITIONAL READINGS FOR CHAPTER 4

Gellerman, Saul W., MOTIVATION AND PRODUCTIVITY (New York: American Management Association, Inc., 1963).

——————————— , MANAGEMENT BY MOTIVATION (New York: American Management Association, Inc., 1968).

Lawler, Edward E., III, PAY AND ORGANIZATIONAL EFFECTIVENESS: A PSYCHOLOGICAL VIEW (New York: McGraw-Hill Book Company, 1971).

Porter, Lyman W. and Edward E. Lawler, III, MANAGERIAL ATTITUDES AND PERFORMANCE (Homewood, Illinois: Richard D. Irwin, Inc. and The Dorsey Press, 1968).

Vroom, Victor H., WORK AND MOTIVATION (New York: John Wiley and Sons, Inc., 1964).

Chapter 5

MANAGEMENT SYSTEMS
AND THE HUMAN ORGANIZATION

In the Introduction I said that each of the major theorists included in this book sees the organization as a system. But it is Rensis Likert more than any other theorist who describes his picture of the organization system and the relationships among the key variables within it.

Likert thinks of the organization as comprising three types of variables. First, the *causal* variables include the factors that managers shape and alter—such things as organization structure, controls, policies, and leadership behavior. Second, the *intervening* variables include the attitudes, motivations, and perceptions of all of the members. Third, the *end-result* variables include measures of organizational performance such as productivity, costs, and earnings.

The Institute for Social Research at the University of Michigan, under Likert's leadership, has mounted a new program of research which it hopes will show consistent, dependable relationships among leadership, motivational and performance variables over time.[1] This project, the Inter-Company Longitudinal Studies, develops questionnaire and performance data which depict the systems state of an organization over time. The questionnaire which Likert has developed measures a core of items covering both causal and intervening variables. (Everyone in an organization being studied completes the questionnaire.) The questionnaire data graphically portray what Likert calls the "management system"—the cluster of factors including structure, controls, policies, and leadership behavior, plus the attitudes, motivations and perceptions of the members. End-result performance variables—productivity, costs, earnings—are also measured.

---

[1] See Rensis Likert and David G. Bowers, "Organizational Theory and Human Resource Accounting," *American Psychologist*, Vol. 24, No. 6 (June 1969), 585-592.

Out of the large number of studies already conducted along these lines by the Institute for Social Research, Likert has identified four types of management systems:

System 1. Exploitive-Authoritative

System 2. Benevolent-Authoritative

System 3. Consultative

System 4. Participative Group.

The gist of Likert's thesis is that particular management systems are consistently associated with certain patterns of performance results over time. He expressed the idea cautiously in a technical article: "The available and growing evidence justifies the view that further research very probably will demonstrate strong and consistent relationships among the causal, intervening, and end-result variables; that [my italics] *certain leadership styles and management systems consistently will be found more highly motivating and yielding better organizational perform-ance than others.* "[2] Specifically, System 4 appears to be consistently associated with more effective performance, System 1 with less effective performance.

Studies of individual companies over several years show that as the management system shifts from a lower to a higher number, performance of the organization improves.[3] Changes in the causal and intervening variables preceed changes in the end-result variables. The time lag appears to vary according to organizational size, type of work, and organizational complexity. The larger or the more complex organization has a greater time lag.

Likert's work makes an important contribution to management thinking. The old-fashioned administrative management theory, as was implied in the Introduction, seemed to posit a direct linear relationship between administrative action and organization end-results. Likert's model offers the concept of intervening variables and also suggests that end-results feed back to both the causal and intervening variables.

Another important idea in the Likert scheme is that in tabulating the financial performance records of any firm, such hitherto uncounted assets as the firm's human organization, its customer loyalty, its shareholder loyalty, its supplier loyalty, its reputation among the financial community, and its reputation in the community in which it has plants and offices should be measured. Some rough methods are in use for estimating the value of the firm's human organiza-

[2] *Ibid.*, p. 591.

[3] Rensis Likert, *The Human Organization: Its Management and Value* (New York: McGraw-Hill Book Company, 1967).

tion.[4] They usually yield a value of three to five times payroll or fifteen to twenty times earnings. There is, in Likert's view, great need for a more comprehensive kind of accounting than we have now because, "When all forms of human resources are ignored in a firm's accounting reports, as at present, the stated earnings can show a favorable picture for several years when the actual assets and true value are steadily *decreasing* by a substantial fraction."[5]

The second article, by Marvin Weisbord, is an interview with Likert and David Bowers, Likert's colleague at the Institute for Social Research. They discuss their work, and their comments illustrate and clarify their theoretical scheme and its practical use.

Here are some questions to guide your study of these articles. All of the theorists we have studied, including Likert, directly or indirectly attach great importance to the participative management style because they believe it to be linked with human satisfaction and organizational effectiveness. How is participative management supposed to contribute to those results? How would Likert answer that question? Why do so many managers seem to practice Systems 1, 2, and 3 if System 4 is better? If the end-result variables feed back into the causal and intervening variables, how do we know that such end-results as satisfaction and productivity aren't the cause of managerial behavior rather than managerial behavior the cause of satisfaction and productivity? That is, might not good performance and good morale in an organization cause a manager to become less directive and controlling and more participative in dealing with his subordinates rather than participative leadership style causing good performance and good morale?

---

[4] For a discussion of what is believed to be the first human resource accounting system in use, see R. Lee Brummet, William C. Pyle, and Eric C. Flamholtz, "Human Resource Accounting In Industry," *Personnel Administration*, Vol. 32, No. 4 (July-August 1969), 34-46.

[5] Likert and Bowers, *op. cit.*, 588.

Human Resources—
The Hidden Assets
Of Your Firm

Rensis Likert

By ignoring a large proportion of their assets, many industries often make sizeable errors in their own financial statements.

These assets include the loyalty and effectiveness of their human organization. They also include supplier loyalty, shareholder loyalty, customer loyalty, and the firm's reputation in the community. But none of these assets is represented in the balance sheet—and virtually no firms keep rigorous quantitative surveillance over them in order to learn whether they are increasing in value from year to year, and by how much.

A crude estimate can be obtained of the value of the human organization of a firm by asking:

"Suppose that tomorrow morning that ——— (the firm) had all of its plants, office, laboratories, warehouses, stores, and all of its equipment—everything, but no personnel except for one person, namely, the president of the firm, and suppose that he had to start rebuilding the human organization of the firm back to where it is today: a well-knit, effectively functioning human organization. How much would it cost expressed in terms of payroll? Would it require one-half year's payroll, one year's, two year's, five year's, or ten year's payroll? What would the total cost be of recruiting, hiring, training, and organization building to rebuild the organization to its present level of effectiveness?"

Estimates by hundreds of company presidents and top managers based on start up costs and other evidence yield figures ranging from two to ten times payroll. The most frequent estimates are three to five times payroll. The complexity of the technology of the industry influences these estimates in that the more complex the technology, the larger the estimates tend to become.

Reprinted from *Credit and Financial Management*, Vol. 71, No. 6 (June, 1969), 20-22, by permission of the author and the National Association of Credit Management.

PAYROLL VS HUMAN WORTH

Let us assume that the human organization of the enterprise is worth twice the annual payroll. For such firms, a ratio of payroll to net earnings, after taxes, of roughly 10 to one appears to be typical. For such firms, their human organization, therefore, is worth twenty times their net earnings (human organization = 2 x payroll = 2 x 10 x earnings).

Since these firms rarely keep careful surveillance over the value of their human organization by means of rigorous quantitative measurements, 10% or even 20% fluctuation upward or downward in the value of the firm's human organization can occur and go undetected by top management and boards of directors.

This means that an able company president, who manages so as to increase the productive capability and hence the value of the firm's human organization in a year (by 5%) is actually achieving earnings twice as large as the figure reported on the balance sheet. Such behavior by a company president is not now recognized nor rewarded. Several years usually elapse before his contribution is realized.

Conversely, it is equally possible for the top management of a firm to report as earnings a cash flow which comes in part or almost entirely from liquidation of part of the value of the firm's human organization. Ruthless pressure in the form of budget cuts, personnel limitations, tightened work standards, and similar steps can maintain or increase cash flow. This is treated at present as earnings in the accounting reports. The decrease in the performance capability of the human organization, however, is usually greater than the increased cash flow since the liquidation of the human organization usually yields in cash only a fraction of the assets liquidated.

Recent progress in social science research has developed the methods which enable any firm which wishes to do so to maintain surveillance over the value of its human organization. Perioric measurements can be obtained which yield information of useful accuracy indicating whether the value of the human organization is remaining about the same or is increasing or decreasing a little or a great deal. At present it is not possible to attach dollar estimates of the amount of shift when an increase or decrease occurs, but we expect to be able to do this in a preliminary way in another few years or so.

Two major research accomplishments in recent years enable the measurements to be made which reveal trends in the productive capability, and therefore the value, of a firm's human organization. First, we have learned what to measure to tell us whether the human organization is becoming more or less effective and second, we have developed the methodology and instruments to measure the relevant variables.

The methodology used is fundamentally different from the usual employee opinion survey. Such opinion surveys typically reveal whether the organization has a fever and how serious it is, but all too often they do not reveal the causes of the fever and what steps to take to correct the undesirable situation. Often they point to symptoms associated with the fever but, as many firms have learned, treating the symptom does not always cure the cause.

VARIABLES DEFINED

To assess correctly the state of the human organization, it is necessary to differentiate between causal and intervening variables. These can be defined briefly as follows:

1. The *causal* variables are independent variables which can be directly or purposely altered or changed by the organization and its management and which, in turn, determine the course of developments within an organization and the results achieved by the organization. "General business conditions," for example, although an independent variable, is *not* viewed as causal since the management of a particular enterprise can do little about them. Causal variables include the structure of the organization, and management's policies, decisions, business leadership strategies, skills, and behavior.

2. The *intervening* variables reflect the internal state, health, and performance capabilities of the organizations, e.g., the loyalties, attitudes, motivations, performance goals, and perceptions of all members and their collective capacity for effective action, interaction, communication, and decision making.

We are finding when we measure key causal variables, such as the extent to which a manager is seen by his subordinates as behaving supportively, that we can predict trends in productivity and cost performance two years in advance. For example, differences in the extent to which department managers in a continuous process plant behaved supportively or built cooperative teamwork among their subordinates in the early part of 1966 was responsible for approximately one-half the variation in cost performance against standards among departments in the early part of 1968.

These and other results indicate that we can assess with useful accuracy whether the human organization of a firm is becoming more or less productive. In addition, we can do much more with what we are now able to measure.

Let me illustrate. We have measured the managerial behavior of thousands of managers and we find that the highest producing managers in American business differ significantly, on the average, from the low producing managers in the principles and procedures they use in managing their human organization. We have been able, moreover, to integrate the principles of managerial behavior used by the highest producing managers into a general theory or system of management. For convenient reference, we are calling this more productive system of management System 4.

MANAGERIAL BEHAVIOR PROGRAM

We are using our knowledge of what to measure and how to measure it in conjunction with System 4 in cooperation with several companies to help them develop and use an especially effective program of organizational development. This involves providing each manager at periodic intervals with measurements of his managerial behavior as seen by his subordinates. These measurements of the causal and intervening variables for the personnel reporting to him reveal to him the strengths and weaknesses in his managerial behavior. By comparing these measurements with standards based on System 4, each manager can diagnose for himself what his problems are and what kinds of changes he needs to make in his managerial behavior to achieve the improvement he may seek. Usually it is advantageous to have available for use by managers, if they wish them, resources to counsel them or help them develop new skills so as to modify their managerial behavior in the desired direction.

We are finding that our capability to measure causal and intervening variables is enabling us also to do the following:

1. Predict one to three years in advance the probable trends, unless deliberate efforts are made to change these trends, in the productivity, costs, earnings, and labor relations of a firm or any department or sub-unit within the firm.

2. Diagnose the causes of the predicted trends and, in so far as these trends are unfavorable, specify the corrective steps to be taken to bring about desired changes.

3. Assess rapidly, and at an early stage, the relative effectiveness of corrective steps which are taken to bring about desired changes and improvements in undesirable trends.

4. If this early assessment of corrective steps reveals that the desired improvement is not being achieved, the measurements can be used to discover what other steps are likely to bring about the desired improvement.

PRODUCTIVITY DATA

As the above uses of the measurement of the causal and intervening variables indicate, they can be used to give management, especially top management, valuable lead time. Data on productivity, costs, scrap, waste, earnings, grievances, and similar end result variables are extremely valuable. But note that all of these data are after the fact measurement. When these variables reflect adverse shifts, all too often serious costs or consequences have already been experienced by a firm.

The great merit of measurements of the causal and intervening variables is that they provide substantial lead time over the end result variables in enabling management to recognize problems and trends and to cope with them or capitalize on them promptly. The measurement of the causal and intervening variables for every manager and supervisor in a firm can provide every level of management substantially greater lead time than now available in recognizing and acting on its strengths and weaknesses in managing its human organization.

FULL MAGNITUDE VARIES

We do not yet know the full magnitude of the lead time which measurements of the causal and intervening variables will provide a firm's manager, and especially its top management. The lead time will be much longer for very large firms than for small firms. It is likely also to vary by the complexity of the technology of the firm. It is likely to be appreciably more than one year for most firms and for very large ones may even be as great as a decade.

We also do not yet know the magnitude of improvement in earnings which an effective shift to System 4 management will bring to a firm. Our preliminary findings indicate that it may be appreciable.

Management
In Crisis

Marvin R. Weisbord

An unprepossessing, Wyoming-born psychologist, Dr. Rensis Likert, since 1947 has been director of the nation's largest academic social science research center—the Institute for Social Research at the University of Michigan. A trim, long-faced man with hollow cheeks, baleful eyes, a thin voice and a gentle smile, "Ren" Likert, now 66, heads an impressive complex, with an overflowing six-story building, a budget pushing $7 million, a payroll over 900, and an annual growth rate of 15 to 20%.

In 1961, Likert attempted to pull out of the welter of studies since World War II a coherent description of what the most productive managers did that their less-productive associates did not do (*New Patterns of Management*, McGraw-Hill). He deduced four modes of behavior which, when carried on in concert, seem to have equal validity for managers as for parents *vis-a-vis* children, and might be summed up as effective leadership. The top producers:

1. Lend lots of support, personal and otherwise, to those doing the job.

2. Facilitate the job with tools, materials, training, outside help, or whatever is needed to get it done.

3. Encourage talk, interaction, mutual help among all members of the work groups.

4. Expect high performance standards all the time.

Likert argued that management really is a system—that structure, policies, practices, and behavior in an organization are closely related to one another, and

Reprinted from *The Conference Board Record,* Vol. 7, No. 2 (February, 1970), 10-16, by permission of the publisher.

that these relationships can be measured. He described four illustrative patterns, from System 1 (an authoritarian dictator decides everything) to System 4 (managerial groups solve policy and operating problems by consensus). His findings showed that the System 1 manager has poorer communication, less confidence, less loyalty, lower motivation, and higher resistance to company goals from his employees than the System 3 or 4 manager, who tended to consult others, listen to their problems, delegate responsibility, provide tools and support, and help people set high goals for themselves.

Likert maintains that people would rather compete against their own best group efforts than against one another. He argues that such competition can lead to greater satisfaction and higher output. But how do you get people working toward self-betterment? First, said Likert, you need the "data." A born quantifier, Likert suggests that managers tend to operate with only about half the data they should have. They count buildings, land, equipment, and cash to the penny, but the value of people, despite rote lip service, is never counted at all.

The innovative approach to management information, which Likert lays out in *The Human Organization* (McGraw-Hill, 1967) may be an important breakthrough in the continuing endeavor to make organization life more rational and satisfying. Over-simplifying a complex theory, there are, says Likert, three kinds of "variables" an organization can measure:

Its management structure and behavior ("causal")
Employee attitudes and motivation ("intervening")
Productivity and earnings ("end result")

Most businesses, Likert holds, measure only the end product—profits. They would never think to measure the effects, good or bad, of their own managerial behavior, for example, on employee motivation. Human resource management, then, is left to chance and considered a frill to be dealt with only after the serious business of profits has been tended to.

Yet, as research from Michigan and elsewhere has begun to suggest, by measuring "causal" and "intervening" variables too, business can predict what costs and profits will be—two, three, four years later. Oddly enough, however, only a handful of bold companies have made any effort to apply Likert's findings. Much of his work is not well-understood nor widely practiced.

There seems, in fact, to be a profound resistance to new technology and ideas in the area Likert has explored. Most executives simply do not believe that it is possible to operate their human systems more productively, especially by permitting more employee influence in decisions, and they often see this as usurpation of control. Moreover, even when confronted with "the data," many executives—as the following interview makes clear—refuse to believe it.

This interview with Dr. Likert was taped in his office a few days before he left for Hawaii, where he is working on a new book about the management of conflict. Dr. David G. Bowers, one of ISR's veteran project directors in business and industrial research, also sat in.   (M. R. W.)

Weisbord: Ren, in *New Patterns* you made the startling statement that many so-called "profit improvement" efforts really were a "liquidation of human assets." You said what seemed like lowered cost was really improved cash flow at the expense of valuable human resources not easily replaced. What led you to that conclusion?

Likert: The first clue was an experiment we did in the early 1950's that didn't yield the expected results. We worked with two clerical departments in a large company. In one, decision-making was pushed to the top. We got them to use the classical scientific-management, work-study approach—cut "deadwood," set standards, pressure everybody to produce at 100% of standard. In the second, they pushed decision-making down, got people involved in setting their own standards. We expected the second department, where people were more highly motivated, to pass the first in productivity within a year.

Weisbord: Did it?

Likert: No. The first was more productive. From previous studies, we knew that the highest-producing managers set high goals, gave their people plenty of support, smoothed the way so goals could be met, used group problem-solving. Here, after a year, just the opposite behavior was getting better results. Yet our measurements showed that the management system was actually deteriorating— the people were demotivated, less loyal, more apt to leave—while the other department's system was improving. Where was the productivity coming from?

It has to be a liquidation of human assets—converting motivation, job commitment, company loyalty—the things consistently high-producing managers capitalize on—into cash. We guessed they couldn't keep it up. But the company was moving its offices around, and we had to break off the study after one year.

Weisbord: What was it confirmed your hunch, then?

Likert: A strange coincidence, really. Floyd Mann was studying a nationwide package delivery company in the mid-50's. He analyzed the leadership patterns, then worked with the worst region to improve performance. The manager was about to be fired, and he was being compared with the three most ably-managed regions in the area. The cards were stacked against us.

But Floyd worked vigorously with the region manager and his local plant managers, trying to teach them what a supervisor had to do to build confidence—listen to problems, help on the job, and so on. They really wanted to improve, and Floyd expected results in six months. When he measured again, some 40 items on his questionnaire response had shifted favorably, showing improved management behavior, but none were statistically significant. And production wasn't up.

Floyd was disappointed. He thought the project had failed. But he kept in touch and brought two fellows into the company who continued to work with the region, helping them improve. One day, about three-and-a-half years later, Floyd was in the regional manager's office and saw a trend chart on the wall. "What's that?" he asked. "It's our cost per package delivered." There was the evidence—down, down, down, starting right about the time Floyd had quit.

So Floyd got the data on costs from the control regions, and he compared them to this region week by week for three or four years. The region where we had worked had shifted from worst to best in cost performance over about a year-and-a-half, and it continued beyond that. And the manager, who had almost lost his job, was now viewed as the most successful regional manager in the area. What we learned from this was that our measurements of improved managerial behavior really did predict better performance—but at a much later time. But we didn't understand it then.

Weisbord: If the findings are so much better understood now, why do many companies continue to respond to a profit decline by putting on a cost squeeze at the expense of employee motivation?

Likert: Well, the top managements of large corporations weren't paying much attention to these findings, even their own. As I looked at the data coming out of GE, IBM, AT&T, and from studies at MIT and Yale, I saw them getting the same message we were. The managers who were more concerned with people and production got better results than the fellows who were oriented toward production alone. But they weren't changing their leadership styles. In the 1950's you had two recessions, and management began to tighten up to retain their earnings.

Weisbord: What kinds of things were done?

Likert: Well, take one large manufacturing company which decentralized just after World War II. It gave 145 independent managers authority to do whatever they thought necessary to get increased earnings. They went like a house afire, and their bonuses were tied to current earnings. If they pushed up earnings, they made a nice fat killing. So they put the screws on. Then came a recession, earnings dropped, and the word came down from on high: make 5% or else. A year or two later 50 or 60 of those top managers were gone. They couldn't make it. They had liquidated their own human assets to get short-term earnings and big bonuses; but that hadn't built the kind of human organization that can respond quickly to cost pressure and belt-tightening.

Actually, we know from other studies going back to the 50's that the more people feel under unreasonable pressure to produce, the lower their productivity, on the average, and the poorer their performance over time. Low-producing units tend to feel under more pressure than high-producing units. They have more absenteeism, turnover, strikes—things of that nature.

Weisbord: What's the relationship there?

Likert: Well, for one thing, when you time jobs, set standards, and pressure people to operate at 100% of standard, you increase the hostility of employees toward one another. You create an authoritarian system. You pit peer against peer. Six months or a year of this, and these guys say, "We're being had. Why the heck should I compete with you? It isn't going to do us any good. Nuts to that." So they begin to find subtle ways to resist that pressure—restrict output, increase grievances, unionize or wildcat strikes if they have a union.

Weisbord: Can you cite some specific examples?

Likert: Oh, sure. One company designed an experiment for us without our even having to do anything. We were studying three of its plants, two small, one large. No sooner had we taken our first measurements than they brought in a consulting firm to do "profit improvement" in one of the small plants. They cut the work force 25%. That was their cost reduction program. It was the plant our measurements showed had the worst management system, so it was no surprise costs were high. Meantime, we started training and development activities in the other two plants to see if we couldn't improve them.
    While we were training, the company also started its cost cutting program in the big plant. When we came back to measure how employees saw the organization and management systems a year later, the management of the first plant, which was pretty bad to begin with, had actually deteriorated. It was worse than before. But the company claimed it had saved $250,000.

Bowers: That's right. The result of the cost reduction was that the organization went to pot. Communications, for example, declined drastically. In this plant our studies showed that communicatons measures forecast cost performance two years later. They would be raising costs at least a million dollars, but they wouldn't see it right away. They didn't pay any attention to that data. And they're paying in terms of productivity for this furious cost reduction they had.

Weisbord: How do you figure that?

Bowers: We know the relationship between our measures and cost performance. Not only were communications poorer, but they were producing less product per man hour. They cut costs in the sense of laying out less money for labor than they used to. But they're also getting less product than they used to from the people who are left.

Weisbord: What happened in the other two plants?

Bowers: We had already done some development work in the big plant before they brought in the cost reduction program. The evidence is that productivity didn't get any better in that plant, but the system didn't deteriorate as much either. On the other hand, the union had been cooperating with the company in some innovative experiments in wages and benefits, and after the cost business the union leadership was voted out of office.

In the third plant the top management did nothing. They left the plant alone and last summer, when I talked to the manager, he told me performance had turned around. They were improving without a "profit improvement" program. But keep in mind that this gain was not visible during the year to two years our study actually was going on.

Weisbord: I guess you need a lot of faith in your people if you aren't going to see results right now. Yet, I've seen companies come right in with the pressure tactics as soon as they get in a cost bind, even though they know they had to ease off last time when it became plain they couldn't hold or attract enough people to keep going. I wonder why? Maybe it's because they have no precedent for behaving differently.

Bowers: There are several forces at work, I think. One is the promotional route in business. Most men in top management today came up through the hardware or money side of the business. They understand physical assets: plant, equipment, cash, and so on. They know how to manipulate symbols, but they don't understand the human organization very well, and the role it plays. They tend to see people as interchangeable. Throw the extra ones you've got out the door. They're surplus. We don't have to replace them.

Moreover, they can be rewarded for that. Make a short-run profit, and you move quickly to a bigger job. If we passed a law tomorrow that every manager had to stay put where he is for the next 10 years, you'd find a substantial shift, I think. The fact that a guy can create a short-term bonus for himself and a long-term mess for his successor, then get promoted and run away from it, allows him to make a career of it. In a way, competent managers are self-selected out because they continually inherit the mess, whereas the guy who created the mess promotes himself to the top—at the expense of the productive capability of the organization.

Likert: Yes, and the interesting thing is that if you ask a group of managers, they'll say time and again, "People are our most valuable asset." But it's double-talk. They don't know what people are worth. I've asked thousands of managers, all over the world, how much it would cost to recruit and build the kind of human organization they have now from scratch. They consistently put it at about three times payroll or more. Last year payrolls averaged about eight times earnings, so you can see that the human organization, on a conservative basis, is worth 24 or 25 times earnings. *That* is what is being liquidated.

A firm could have a 10 or 20% fluctuation in the value of its human organization from year to year and never know it. An able president, who increases the productive capacity, hence the value, of his human organization by only 5% would be achieving earnings *double* the figure on the balance sheet. The way things stand now his behavior would neither be recognized nor rewarded.

Weisbord: Okay, but suppose the emergency is real. You've got to move fast to stay solvent. If your studies show that pressure produces profits in the short run, wouldn't I be better off applying pressure if I need a quick shot in the arm?

Likert: No. The corporation's better off if it sells inventory, or a plant, or real estate. It's easier to replace inventory than to rebuild an organization.

Weisbord: Well then why don't more managers do it?

Likert: Because companies watch inventory. They watch plant maintenance. They account for it. But they don't watch the human organization, or customer relations, or community reputation. So the manager says, "If I have to cut back, I'll cut where they aren't watching. Where they watch me, I behave myself." He'd cut back R&D, except that top management watches R&D. If they couldn't count the cash box, he'd use cash. Managers will cut costs in any area the company doesn't keep under surveillance.

Bowers: There's stockholders influence too. A manager fáced with a crisis can go before the stockholders and say, "Well, we've cut down expenses by laying off so-and-so many people, and we've preserved your investment." Their investment is the physical side. Suppose he'd said, "Well, we've sold the plant and we sold the inventory and we got rid of some patents, but we've still got our staff." Actually, they probably have more investment in the human organization than they have in the equipment. It really makes more sense to cash in physical assets which are readily replaced anyway—a marginal plant, old equipment, and so on. But stockholders don't see it that way.

Weisbord: Okay, now suppose I have no physical assets to sell? I'm pared to the bone already. Then what do I do?

Bowers: You could do what Harwood Manufacturing did when it merged with Weldon Manufacturing back in 1962. They didn't realize the extent of the human problems. They thought they could leave marketing alone, bring in some new equipment and spruce up the plant, and be in fine shape. It didn't work that way. There was major conflict between manufacturing and marketing. Orders were being goofed up. Productivity was very low. Weldon was holding customers only by a complicated system of advertising allowances that amounted to selling the product at a loss. It was a mess. And the screws already were on as tight as could be.

Weisbord: Yes, I remember that from the book you did with Marrow and Seashore.[1] Would you want to review briefly the strategy Harwood followed?

Bowers: It has three parts. First, communicate your ideals and principles to the other organization. Second, make the technology adequate to the job you want them to do. Finally, change the social side of the organization to match the technology.

Weisbord: What were some of the specific changes they made to cut costs? Did they fire people?

Bowers: No. Keep in mind they changed the technology, and that led to a whole array of changes. But they also used sensitivity training in "family" groups—supervisors, assistants, mechanics, and so on. Then they taught supervisors how to use problem-solving techniques with hourly employees. How to sit groups down in a room, for example, and ask them what things they felt kept them from doing their jobs more effectively. These were posted on long sheets of newsprint.

Weisbord: What kinds of things did the employees come up with?

Bowers: Mostly the kind related to work, like asking for job re-assignment, or setting up systems so people who weren't coming in would let their supervisors know. And work methods. "Why can't we use a different kind of thread on such-and-such garment? It's easier to handle." That sort of thing. And the company responded to every item, either doing it right away, in which case employees saw immediate change they had influenced, or explaining why they couldn't and whether or not it would be practical in the future. They solved a lot of cost problems that way.

Weisbord: As I recall, there were some dramatic improvements in all sorts of ways.

Bowers: That's right. Within two years turnover went down 60%, absenteeism was down 50%, and incentive earnings had risen 16%. Return on invested capital went from minus 15% to plus 17%. Of course, Harwood had a lot of experience at this sort of thing. Some of the change was due to improved technology. But it also matched a shift in management from System 1 to well over towards System 4.

Weisbord: I wonder whether anybody but a pioneer like Harwood, which knew what to do and how to do it, could do likewise and get similar results.

Likert: Well, one of the curious things is that we keep running into "natural" System 4 managers. After all, we didn't invent the most effective system. We deduced it by watching what the consistent high producers do. Almost every company has some of these. The trouble is top management doesn't always recognize what they do as legitimate, or necessary. A lot of managers think that if you meet people's needs on the job you're "coddling" them, and that this hurts productivity and control.

I remember a few years ago one well-known company, with plants all over the country, started timing jobs, introducing work standards, getting production up. All the plants were ordered to do this, but one manager said "no." Only one. The division president went down there and ordered this manager to do it. He said, "I won't. I tried that 10 years ago and it won't work." He resisted top management, and he got away with it.

Weisbord: How did he do that?

Likert: Let me back up a minute. Before I heard this story, I had talked to a personnel staff man in that company, and he said, "Ren, your findings and conclusions make sense in all our plants except one. Our highest producing plant is run by a System 1 manager. He puts great pressure on his employees for high performance and keeps getting it. I wish you'd go down there and look at it and tell me what gives."

Weisbord: Did you go?

Likert: Yes. A year later I went down with the corporate personnel man, and we walked in just before lunch. The local manager was pretty careful what he said to the people from New York. We went out in the plant. It was beautifully engineered, impressive. But the interesting thing is that it was not laid out by industrial engineers. I asked how they set quotas or goals. The manager said, "we ask each manager to suggest his department's goals for the next quarter. He asks his people where and how they can improve procedures and do a better job and cut costs." Fundamentally, it was group decision-making.

As we walked around, I noticed people seemed relaxed, and there were transistor radio going all over the place. How come? "Oh, there's a local high school basketball game on." I spent the next morning with this "high pressure" manager. I had a whole bunch of questions. How about performance review? He said, "I don't like it. I prefer to spend the same time and money training our supervisors on how to interview, how to listen." He himself would constantly interview people in the plant to see where the problems were and what was causing them and what they thought should be done about them. He took a standard company training program and shifted it to where they were teaching supervisors problem-solving, using actual work problems. He was using group problem-solving with his own people. Emphasizing supportive behavior. I could give you all sorts of examples.

Weisbord: How did he come to this?

Likert: It made sense to him. He got results. One principle he lived by was this: "There is no policy or procedure we will not change if we can't explain it to people in the plant in a way that makes sense. If we can't make sense out of it, we'll change it." That's how they got the transistors. The people said others had Muzak. They wanted radios. He said, "Okay, if it won't interfere with production." Corporate headquarters is still raising cain about that.

One thing. He was no-nonsense on productivity. He had high performance goals, and he believed in rewarding people for productivity. Time clocks, he said, were a mess. He set up an experiment, measured attitudes, then threw out the clocks. They have a salary system. Straight salary. If you increase productivity, and hold it for three months, you get an increase in pay. And you keep it, even if you drop back later. You just don't get further increases. He promoted from within too. When a job opened up, the guy who was highest producing on the job below had first choice.

You ask his subordinates to fill out a questionnaire, and he's way over at System 4. The irony was that when he tried to describe his leadership style at the company executive development school, everybody said, "Well, it's okay for him. That's his personality. Nothing here I can use. Doesn't apply to me."

To this day top management doesn't realize this man's management principles are worth at least 5% of the company's total payroll, because virtually every one of their thousands of managers could improve his performance using them. Instead, he'll retire and the firm will never know what a great asset slipped through its fingers! No wonder he wouldn't let them bring in pressure tactics.

Weisbord: If my company were in a profit squeeze, and I didn't want to destroy my human assets to get out of it, but I wasn't a "natural" System 4 manager either, what would I do?

Likert: First of all, you have to recognize every employee wants his company to be financially successful. He wants a secure job. He wants pay increases and promotions. That calls for financial success. If your company's in trouble, every employee's concerned about it. It's very feasible to go to your people and say, "Look, we're heading for trouble. Productivity isn't as high as it should be. To stay competitive we've got to sell a good product at a favorable price, and other companies are developing better ways of doing the job. What shall we do?"

Weisbord: In other words, share the problem with the employees. Use your human assets, don't liquidate them. A lot of managers would say that would only scare employees unnecessarily.

Likert: They'll be a lot more scared when the heads begin to roll. This way, they have a chance to help. They don't feel powerless under pressure. Remember what Harwood did at Weldon. You can start using productive problem-solving. Ask people what work standards ought to be. If they don't know, then time the job. Tell them what's considered par, and ask them if they think it's too high or too low. But let *them* set the standards, and let them know that the company's success, therefore their future, depends on coming up with better methods of working.

You can set up a task force in every department and say, "Look, we'll give you any resource you want. Technical, financial, engineering, outside consultants—whatever you need to help you re-organize the job in ways that will enable us to cut costs. Work smarter, not harder. Cut out the wasteful activities."

You can do it in a crisis situation. Instead of getting outside consultants to superimpose change, have it come from within. You may have to do a little coaching. You may have to bring in skill-training in group process and problem-solving. You may have to teach people to listen to each other. You may need new kinds of measurements to diagnose your strengths and weaknesses. We know how to do that now—with questionnaires, video tapes, counseling, observing and reporting on meetings, feeding back data. There are all kinds of things.

Weisbord: Okay, but what about the comment you hear all the time: That's fine for some companies, or certain kinds of employees, or particular industries. But not *mine.* My problem is unique, and I could never do these things with my people.

Likert: We've seen production go up in chemical process plants, insurance companies, oil companies, a company that makes mirrors. We've got fascinating data from Japan and Yugoslavia, too. In Yugoslavia, we took 10 pairs of plants, each pair making identical products, each about the same size, but one high-producing and the other average. In every pair, the high-producing plant is more toward System 4. Same thing in Japan. Heck, we have data from India, Pakistan, Sweden too. Beer salesmen in Sweden. The more the supervisors use System 4, the more beer the salesmen sell. But if you don't think it applies to you, the best answer is, "Collect the data. Find out what the differences are between your own high- and low-producing departments."

Weisbord: I think you're saying that System 4 has to do with basic human principles, the conditions under which most people most of the time do a better job.

Likert: That's right. The whole problem of how man relates to man is a learned process. It was pretty primitive in cave-man times, less so in early tribal days, a little less so in feudal times, and still less so in the early days of the industrial revolution. And it's better still today. For tens of thousands of years man has been learning to live and work with his fellow man. We've been studying what the highest-producing managers in business and government do. What we're finding is a more sophisticated, a more complex way for men to work together productively than ever before.

Weisbord: And you're suggesting that this way, what you sum up as System 4, is the best we know so far?

Likert: Yes, it's better for mental health, physical health, satisfaction, and productive work. But you've got to have high performance goals too. You can't run it like a country club. Furthermore, as this research continues, and businesses become more innovative, we're going to find a new System 5 that will out-perform System 4.

Weisbord: Where will that come from?

Likert: Out of the System 4 companies. What are their problems? What things do they want changed? How can they improve? Where does the data show they have weaknesses in their human organization? How can they make better use of their human capabiliites?

We're already seeing changes in company structure, in policies, in decision-making, in ways of rewarding people. And we're still figuring out better ways to measure all this. We don't know yet the magnitude of improved earnings that a shift toward System 4 will bring to a firm, let alone a System 5. But our preliminary findings indicate that it may be considerable, and much more than most managers would imagine.

REFERENCES

1. *Management By Participation*, by Alfred J. Marrow, David G. Bowers, and Stanley E. Seashore (Harper & Row, 1967).

ADDITIONAL READINGS FOR CHAPTER 5

Caplan, Edwin H., MANAGEMENT ACCOUNTING AND BEHAVIORAL SCIENCE (Reading, Massachusetts: Addison-Wesley Publishing Company, 1971).

Likert, Rensis, NEW PATTERNS OF MANAGEMENT (New York: McGraw-Hill Book Company, 1961).

——————————— , THE HUMAN ORGANIZATION (New York: McGraw-Hill Book Company, 1967).

Marrow, Alfred J., David G. Bowers, and Stanley E. Seashore, MANAGEMENT BY PARTICIPATION (New York: Harper and Row, Publisher, 1967).

Chapter 6

ORGANIZATION DEVELOPMENT

Despite certain differences, the several theories we have studied show an overriding consensus. Their policy implications, particularly, all point in the same direction. Organizations should use participative management to develop clear and realistic goals and controls. Organizations should design jobs which provide feelings of achievement and rewards which reinforce performance (although some theorists deemphasize money as a motivator). Whether the key phrase is Theory Y or System 4, the message is much the same.

Likert speaks for all, I believe, when he says that organizations need better interaction-influence systems that now exist.[1] Multiple, overlapping, group inter-action-influence systems are required to permit organizations to cope success-fully with the kinds of problems they face. Specifically, organizations need to assist leaders and members in developing cooperative relations, achieving high-level performances, and resolving conflicts. Organizations need to develop quick responses to turbulent environments.

But how can we build better interaction-influence systems within organizations? That is the central concern of the writers in this chapter. Their premise, implicit or explicit, is that groups are the key, that better management of inter-personal events and processes is the way to make organizations more satisfying and productive. They discuss the planned use of behavioral science-based techniques for intervening in interpersonal processes to make better organizations. This special activity is called organization development, or OD for short.

Warren Bennis, the author of the first article, believes that bureaucracy, the type of organization which served so well in the past, is ill-suited to the present

---

[1] Likert and Bowers, "Organizational Theory and Human Resource Accounting," *American Psychologist*, Vol. 24, No. 6 (June 1969), 585-592.

and to the future. He sees the need to renew organizations as a central social problem. And he sees the making of better organizations as dependent upon changing the beliefs and values of people who interact within organizations. In the OD view, the new values must favor interpersonal honesty, openness, and trust, and support individuality and risk-taking.

Bennis defines organization development as an *educational strategy* adopted to bring about a *planned organizational change.* OD is not the same as sensitivity training, although such training in self-awareness is sometimes used as a step towards building the kind of social awareness which OD seeks to foster among interdependent people in organizations. The tactics of OD are varied. Bennis describes some of them and offers several illustrations.

The second article, by Robert Blake and Jane Mouton, describes their own approach to OD, the managerial grid. The grid is a diagram which portrays a range of management styles,varying in the degree to which the central concern is with production or people. In Blake and Mouton OD seminars, the grid serves to focus managers' attention upon their own values and styles. Participants critique one another's style. Later, work teams explore how to improve their operation. Blake and Mouton believe that the grid approach to OD has helped produce positive results in numerous companies.

The last article, by Chris Argyris, describes the popular laboratory education technique called the T- (for training) group. The T-group puts the participant in the same kind of "learning by doing" situation that college course laboratory sessions create for the students. There are no test tubes or microscopes, however. The subject for study is the ongoing behavior of the participants. The contrived laboratory situation generates behavior which the participants can use to teach themselves about human behavior in organizations. Hopefully, the participants can examine old behavior patterns, experiment with new ones, and attempt to carry over the more effective ones to their organizational roles.

Probably no single topic raises so much controversy, informed and otherwise, as sensitivity training. Why? What conditions would be conducive to the carryover of behavior learned in the laboratory to routine performance in the work organization? When should one not practice interpersonal trust, honesty, openness, and "levelling?" If the organization is an interdependent system of human and structural factors, as we have been saying all along, what alternatives to changing individuals' values directly are conceivable? Are the values and the participative leadership styles these theorists generally favor equally suitable for different types of organizations—organizations having different purposes and technologies? Is it possible to develop a more closely integrated team and still emphasize individuality?

Organization Development: What It Is and What It Isn't

Warren G. Bennis

Organization development (OD) is a response to change, a complex educational strategy intended to change the beliefs, attitudes, values, and structure of organizations so that they can better adapt to new technologies, markets, and challenges, and the dizzying rate of change itself. Organization development is new and still emerging, only a decade old, so its shape and potentiality are far from granted and its problems far from solved. Yet it holds promise for developing the "real knowledge" about our post-modern world.

It might be helpful at the outset to review some examples of organization development and from these illustrations develop a fuller understanding of the subject, rather than starting from an abstract, and perhaps useless, definition.

Example 1. Team Development. Douglas McGregor (1967) was a consultant to a management group at Union Carbide in 1964. One of the explicit tasks of the consultant was to help build an "effective management team." This was defined in terms of a number of features, including: 1) understanding, mutual agreement, and identification regarding the goals of the group, 2) open communication, 3) mutual trust, 4) mutual support, 5) effective management of conflict, 6) developing a selective and appropriate use of the team concept, 7) utilizing appropriate member skills, and 8) developing appropriate leadership. I suppose that these criteria would be shared by most organizations requiring collaborative efforts.

McGregor, along with the formal head of the management group, John Paul Jones, devised a crude scale which represented as closely as possible these features of an effective team (Table 1-1):

Reprinted by permission of the author and the publisher from *Organization Development: Its Nature, Origins, and Prospects* (Reading, Massachusetts: Addison-Wesley Publishing Company, 1969), pp. 2-10, 17.

Table 1-1   Team Development Scale

1. Degree of mutual trust:
   High suspicion   High trust
      (1)   (4)   (7)

2. Communications:
   Guarded, cautious   Open, authentic
      (1)   (4)   (7)

3. Degree of mutual support:

                                                                       Genuine concern
   Every man for himself   for each other
      (1)   (4)   (7)

4. Team objectives:
   Not understood   Clearly understood
      (1)   (4)   (7)

5. Handling conflicts within team:
   Through denial, avoidance,   Acceptance and
   suppression, or compromise   "working through"
      (1)   (4)   of conflicts
                                                                             (7)

6. Utilization of member resourdes:
   Competencies   Competencies
   used by team   not used
      (1)   (4)   (7)

7. Control methods:
   Control is imposed   Control from within
      (1)   (4)   (7)

8. Organizational environment:
   Restrictive, pressure   Free, supportive, respect
   for conformity   for differences
      (1)   (4)   (7)

McGregor (1967, p. 172) writes:

> I have seen groups make effective use of a simple rating scale (like the exhibit above) for purposes of analysis. After a little discussion of the meaning of each variable, each member fills out the form anonymously, rating his personal view of the current state of the group. The ratings are then pooled and a chart prepared by a couple of members showing the mean of the ratings and the high and low 'score' for each variable. On the basis of these data, the group discusses what aspects of its group operation need work.[1]

The main purpose of this exercise, according to McGregor, is to provide each member of the group with feedback about how others perceive the group in relation to himself and feedback about how group effectiveness can be improved.

Example 2. Intergroup Conflict. Among the recent problems facing the U.S. Department of State was unproductive divisiveness between the Foreign Service officers, sometimes referred to as "the club" or "the guild" and the administrative staff of State. The stereotyping and mutual distrust, if not downright hostility, blocked communication and reduced effectiveness enormously, for each "side" perceived the other as more threatening than any realistic overseas enemy.

During a State Department conference held at M.I.T. in early June of 1966, Chris Argyris (1967) and I divided a group of top echelon administrative officers and Foreign Service officers into two groups along functional lines. The two groups were assigned to separate rooms, and were asked to discuss three questions and to develop a list of words or phrases that would summarize their answers:

1. What qualities best describe our group?
2. What qualities best describe the other group?
3. What qualities do we predict the other group would assign to us?

As Argyris (1967, pp. 20-21) wrote:

> The faculty reported that the groups became involved in the exercise and produced products that reflected validly the discussions that were held in their separate meeting rooms.

The results were as follows:
The Foreign Service officers saw themselves as:

1. Reflective
2. Qualitative
3. Humanistic, subjective
4. Cultural, broad interests
5. Generalizers
6. Intercultural sensitivity
7. Detached from personal conflicts

The Foreign Service officers saw the administrative officers as:

1. Doers and implementers
2. Quantitative
3. Decisive and forceful
4. Noncultural

5. Limited goals
6. Jealous of us
7. Interested in form more than substance
8. Wave of the future! (exclamation mark theirs)
9. Drones but necessary evils

The Foreign Service officers predicted that the administrative officers would see them as:

1. Arrogant, snobs
2. Intellectuals
3. Cliquish
4. Resistant to change
5. Inefficient, dysfunctional
6. Vacillating and compromising
7. Effete

The administrative officers saw themselves as:

1. Decisive, guts
2. Resourceful, adaptive
3. Pragmatic
4. Service-oriented
5. Able to get along
6. Receptive to change
7. Dedicated to job
8. Misunderstood
9. Useful
10. Modest! (added by the individual doing the presenting)

The administrative officers saw the Foreign Service officers as:

1. Masked, isolated
2. Resourceful, serious
3. Respected
4. Inclined to stability
5. Dedicated to job
6. Necessary
7. Externally oriented

8. Cautious
9. Rational
10. Surrounded by mystique
11. Manipulative
12. Defensive

The administrative officers predicted that the Foreign Service officers would see them as:

1. Necessary evil
2. Defensive, inflexible
3. Preoccupied with minutiae
4. Negative and bureaucratic
5. Limited perspective
6. Less cultural (educated clerks)
7. Misunderstood
8. Practical
9. Protected
10. Resourceful

After the lists were produced, the two groups assembled together and then proceeded to discuss their lists and to be questioned by the other group with respect to their perceptions. The discussion was intense, high-pitched, noisy, argumentative, good-humored, and finally, several hours later, thoughtful. It appeared as if each side moved to a position where they at least understood the other side's point of view.

Example 3. Confrontation Meeting.   The Director of a small and spectacularly successful educational R&D firm called to see whether I could help their rapidly growing nonprofit enterprise. He felt that the organization had grown too rapidly; that the project teams were not in communication, and worse, were extremely competitive; that the organization had to make some serious decisions regarding its future, especially with respect to whether or not it would produce and market the wonderfully creative things it was inventing for school systems; and besides all this, he felt woefully behind in his own creative work and wondered whether or not his office could be managed more effectively. He also made it clear to me that the people wanted nothing to do with T-groups or sensitivity training. I spent a morning with the Director and his entire professional staff, consisting of some 40 individuals, almost all of them holding PhD's and joint appointments at nearby universities.

Everything that the Director had related to me was confirmed by interviews with the professional staff, except that they found the leadership of the firm too loose and unstructured and too often "invisible." It appeared to me that the Director, though marvelously charismatic, was seen by his staff as spending too much of his time in Washington or at his office at the university or where he could not be reached.

We agreed to spend a full day together in a "confrontation meeting" the following week. The confrontation meeting, invented by Richard Beckhard (see also Beckhard, 1969), seemed ideally suited to this case. The entire group of 40 professionals along with the Director met in a nearby motel for about seven hours. I spent the first half-hour reviewing recent history and setting forth certain elementary generalizations regarding all human organizations. I set forth certain concepts about organizations which they might find helpful in talking about their own. In the next phase, which lasted one hour, the group of 40 was broken into eight groups of five, cutting across all formal organizational lines, and the participants were asked to discuss the "most significant problems they face in getting their job done. What were the de-motivators? What 'bugged' them?" They were asked to return in one hour with a list of their main problems and causes of those problems. The eight groups brought back dozens of pieces of paper (which were festooned along the walls) listing over 200 problems. I then tried to categorize the problems and came up with five major categories:

1. questions of the identity and destiny of the firm,

2. questions about collaboration and competition,

3. questions about authority, influence, and power,

4. questions about competence, and more precisely doubts about other people's competence, and

5. questions about expectations and clarity, like: who expected what from whom?

Each of the 200 or so problems was numbered from one to five, indicating its particular category. After lunch, the individuals were regrouped according to their formal, intact, organizational structure and were asked to spend an hour or so on recommendations they could make to the Director and top management on the main problems that fell within their particular sphere of influence. The Director and his administrative staff worked together during this period. Finally, in the last period of an hour and a half, the groups reassembled and group by group confronted the Director with their recommendations. To summarize, the day went as follows:

9:30 to 10:00   Introduction

10:00 to 11:00   Data collection—problem generation

11:00 to 12:00   Information sharing and categorization
1:30 to   2:45   Priority setting and action planning
2:45 to   4:30   Confrontation and implementation

To provide a more concrete idea of problems, one group listed the following:

Meetings like this should start on time. "Minor irritants," like post-poned meetings, are rarely communicated to people.

The authority structure is unclear. Who's my boss? Who judges my work?

Until recently, there has been little cross-fertilization.

The Director is inaccessible. Members of the power structure are very accessible to some, but Dr. X (Associate Director) doesn't return his calls. As a result, the number of memos has increased.

There is no system of setting priorities on distribution of materials. Does a policy exist? Is it possible to have one?

It is a problem for newcomers to discover who does what in the organization.

There are too many people employed and then not permitted to exercise the skills they were hired for.

Too many meetings are held without a specific agenda.

How do information and decisions that come out of these meetings get communicated?

Taking over responsibility as acting project director has taken me away from my primary interest—this is irritating and annoying.

Difficult to get a sure assessment of peoples' strengths and weaknesses.

Who makes decisions around here?

Funding is chaotic. Whom do we go to for funds?

The recommendations of the staff to the Director were received, if not gratefully, then without rancor and certainly with great concern. As a result of this meeting, more regular and meaningful meetings were held, a clear-cut organizational structure evolved, and most important, the Director felt that he would much rather spend the bulk of his time on substantive matters and decided to relinquish his role to another person in the firm who had administrative ambition and talent.

Example 4. Data Feedback.   Six accounting departments completed surveys concerned with aspects of their organization, work, and human relations. These departments employed about 60 supervisors and 640 nonsupervisory employees.

Four of the departments received knowledge of the results of their questionnaires—"feedback"—in conferences over a 12-month period and were called the
"experimental departments." The other two "control" departments received no
special attention from the management or research group other than the regular
administrative practices. Both before and after the experiment in data feedback,
these departments filled out lengthy questionnaires which covered a wide variety
of attitudes and feelings concerning the major aspects of the work situation. It
should be stressed that the "experimental departments" had intensive discussions for almost a year, discussions which were based on surveys they themselves
had completed.

When the experimental and control groups were compared, it was found that
the groups which experienced the data feedback felt that:

> They were better at getting the job done.
>
> They were freer to take job problems to their supervisors.
>
> Their supervisors better understood their point of view.
>
> Their supervisors got along better with each other.
>
> They understood better how their supervisor sees things.

As the author of the study (Baumgartel, 1959, p. 6) concluded:

> The results of this study suggest that the creative use of new informa-
> tion for conferences and meetings at all levels of departmental organiza-
> tion may be one of the best and most dynamic avenues to management
> development and organizational growth.

Example 5. Elements in a One-Year Program.   In 1960 a small refinery of
about 500 employees with 60 management personnel was on the verge of bank-
ruptcy and practically defunct due to an oversupply of the world's petroleum
resources and special production problems of the refinery. The parent firm had
all but decided to close the refinery but union and political pressures developed,
along with certain changes of policy from headquarters, which led to an attempt
to revitalize the refinery. A new top manager was hired and New York headquarters' staff was brought in to help in the organizational development of the
refinery.

After a management survey was accomplished, intensive feedback sessions
were held with each constituent unit. This was followed by a series of weekly
seminars given by prominent organizational theorists whose main purpose was to
provide a number of models for thinking about organizational change. Following
this, all 60 supervisors participated in a week-long sensitivity training laboratory
where the main emphasis was placed on interpersonal competencies and skills in
intergroup coordination. As a result of these educational ventures, after which

revaluation of needs and rediagnoses were accomplished, a joint committee system for plant-wide participation was achieved along with a modification of the Scanlon labor plan. This was the first time that the Scanlon plan was successfully adapted to a process industry.

CONCLUSION

In conclusion, it might be useful to say a few words about what organization development *is not*. It should be clear by now that organization development is not simply *sensitivity training*. To be sure, many organization-development practitioners rely to a greater or lesser extent on experience-based educational programs, and some variant of sensitivity training is frequently used. But, as I have tried to show, a wide variety of programs can be effective, from data feedback sessions to confrontation meetings. The important thing about organization development is that data are generated from the client system itself. Frequently, these are the only data that count anyway, as there is sufficient evidence that data collected on "others" (no matter how valid) almost always lack the impact of self-generated data.

I hope it is also clear by now that organization development is not another fancier version of "permissive" leadership. Why this myth continues to be perpetuated despite all the experience to the contrary puzzles me. Organization development does not prescribe any particular "style of leadership" other than an open and confronting one, which is anything but "permissive." Nor does it imply a group consensus as the only form of decision-making, though some writers (such as Blake and Mouton) certainly believe that consensus is a natural conclusion given training under the "Managerial Grid" orientation.

The basic value underlying all organization-development theory and practice is that of *choice*. Through focused attention and through the collection and feedback of relevant data to relevant people, more choices become available and hence better decisions are made. That is essentially what organization development is: an educational strategy employing the widest possible means of experience-based behavior in order to achieve more and better organizational choices in a highly turbulent world.

NOTES

1. From *The Professional Manager* by Douglas McGregor. Copyright 1967, McGraw-Hill Book Co., New York. Used with permission of McGraw-Hill Book Co.

REFERENCES

Argyris, C. (1967), *Some Causes of Organizational Ineffectiveness within the Department of State*, Washington, D.C., Department of State.

Baumgartel, H. (1959), "Using employee questionnaire results for improving organizations," *Kansas Business Review*, No. 12, pp. 2-6.

Beckhard, R. (1967), "The confrontation meeting," *Harvard Business Review*, Vol. XLV, No. 2, pp. 149-153.

Beckhard, R. (1969), Organization Development: Strategies and Models, Reading, Mass., Addison-Wesley.

McGregor, D. (1967), *The Professional Manager*, New York, McGraw-Hill.

Organization Excellence
Through Effective
Management Behavior

Robert R. Blake
Jane Srygley Mouton

When the word "moon" is mentioned today, a listener is far less likely to think of green cheese, what the cow jumped over, or June and spoon than about launching pads and space capsules. Just so, "management" no longer conjures up a picture of an ogre, a big rich corporate tycoon, or the "robber barons" so much as the scientific knowledge a modern manager uses to organize his work and work of others.

APPLYING "SCIENCE"

Many new scientific ideas about management have evolved during the past decade from research findings in the behavioral sciences. One new approach to management has been hailed as a scientific "breakthrough" and is being used by many leading companies in the United States and Canada as well as Great Britain, Australia, and Japan. It is known as the Managerial Grid.

The Grid is based on research into practical use of behavioral science in business. It is more than just a theory. It is a framework in which a variety of findings about behavior of managers can be fitted. It is a behavioral road map.

Companies that have used Grid learning say that it has improved management. Some can even show its direct influence on their profit and loss statements. They have realized better output when their managers understand what lies behind their styles of behavior and the effects it has on others. The Grid makes it possible for all managers and whole organizations to learn better ways to manage.

Reprinted from *Manage* Magazine, Vol. 20, No. 2 (1967), 42-47, by permission of the authors and the publisher. Copyright 1967 by The National Management Association.

PHILOSOPHY CHANGE

Until 20 years or so ago, good managers were thought to have a born talent. It took quite a few experiments to discover exactly what it is that makes a good manager. Every man, whether he knows it or not, has deeply imbedded theories about behavior that are reflected in his style of managing. Once a man has a clear, explicit idea or theory about how to manage, a theory about how to work with others, how to integrate people and production, he finds it possible to become a better and better manager in countless ways.

He not only knows how to direct people's work, but how to put to work the good that can come out of the disagreements that invariably arise. He can make conflict useful as well as resolve it. Furthermore, when all managers in a company share ideas about the soundest ways to manage, the work climate takes on

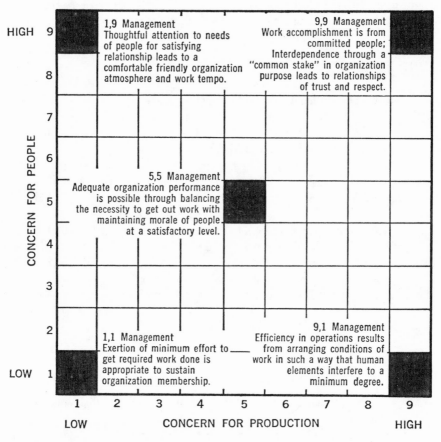

Figure 1   *The managerial grid.*

a whole new atmosphere. It is an atmosphere of fact finding, trust, and confidence among members of the organization, and problem solving by thrashing through problems to resolution, not by simply giving in, horse trading, smoothing over differences, or pushing one's own solutions on a take-it-or-leave-it basis.

WHAT IS IT?

The Grid is an 81-squared framework on which styles of behavior can be plotted. A manager has to think about two things—How to get the work done and the people who are going to do the work. Some managers have production on their minds more than people; others, people more than production. On the horizontal axis of the Grid, which goes from 1 to 9, the 9 represents high concern for output, the 1 low concern for output. On the vertical axis, the 9 represents high concern for people and the 1 low concern for people.

GRID THEORIES USED

In the lower right-hand corner, "9,1" represents a great deal of concern for output but very little for the people who are expected to produce. At the opposite corner of the Grid is "1,9" representing much concern for people and little for the output needed in a healthy business.

Another Grid corner is 1,1. It seems almost impossible that a manager could have little or no concern for either people or production, but these are the ones in an organization who go through the motions of being a part of it but are invisible though present. They are not participators or doers but free-riders. They have not quit the organization, but they have done a mental walkout.

Still another possibility is in dead center of the Grid. This is the 5,5 style. A manager with this approach is on a seesaw. He says to his people, "Let's get to work but don't kill yourself, and don't rush around, but find yourself a comfortable tempo." He tells himself not to push too much or he will be seen as hardnosed, and not to let people off too easy or he will be seen as soft, to be "fair but firm." He is the "organization man."

UPPER RIGHT

The upper right-hand corner, the 9,9 position, denotes a high concern for both production and people and involves some new and useful ideas. A man with a 9,9 orientation emphasizes fact finding for problem solving. When conflict arises, the facts are dug into and thrashed through to solution of a problem. The 9,9 position is characterized by commitment of organization members to accomplishment of work which contributes to organization goals. They recognize an interdependence through a common stake in the outcome of their work.

Furthermore, managers have been found to use at least two theories, a dominant and a backup. Pressure brings out a manager's backup theory. For example, a man may display a 5,5 style most of the time, but when he is under pressure, he may shift to a 9,1 style of managing, calling upon his authoritative backup theory for a way to get something accomplished. Or a man may have a 1,1 backup style. He may function regularly as a 9,1 production oriented manager but backed into a corner, when he is not able to get his own way, he may move down into the "to-heck-with-it-I-quit" 1,1 position. It is a widely recognized fact that fatigue pushes a manager down toward the 9,1 corner and finally into the 1,1 corner. Overindulgence in alcohol is a sure path to 1,1.

HOW CAN IT HELP?

When managers from the same company study the Grid, it gives them two things—a set of ideas for thinking about production-people problems and a language for describing and talking about them. It provides them with ideas for studying their own practices and attitudes and for changing their own behavior. With this framework, an organization's procedures can be revised. Indeed the whole organization culture can be changed to achieve a 9,9 climate.

TEXTBOOK PLUS . . .

The Grid is not learned from a textbook alone. Rather, managers study theories of the Grid in week-long seminars. These seminars include personal study by each man of his managerial style, and measurement of his team effectiveness as he works on a team with others. A high point of the seminar is when each person receives a critique of his managerial style from the other members of his team based on his behavior during the week. The emphasis is on his style of managing, not on his character traits or personality. Another high point is when managers discuss the style of their organization cultures and begin to consider steps for increasing the effectiveness of their companies.

PREWORK INVOLVED

The seminars require about 30 hours of "prework" before the actual study week begins. The seminar usually starts on Sunday afternoon, and participants study morning, noon, and night through noon the following Friday. The seminars are self-taught, since the method of instruction is by instruments—questionnaires and measurement tasks. But the study is not classroom study so much as it is the study of action.

ORGANIZATIONAL BENEFITS

A Grid seminar week is the foundation for six-phase Grid Organization Development, an approach to improving the effectiveness of an entire organization. A second step is to apply learnings back on the job within one's own work team, an on-the-job extension of Grid learning called Work Team Development. Each work team investigates how it works, and decides how to get the most effective 9,9 approach to work problems. It starts with top executives and moves down through the organization. Team members probe for facts, listen, maintain attitudes of self-examination, and get better relationships with one another by facing up to conflict and solving it on the spot. Each man also receives an action critique of how he works from other team members.

The last four phases of Grid Organization Development are built upon the first two. They enable managers to work toward developing the culture and the business practices of the whole organization. In Phase 3 the emphasis shifts from managers to groups in the organization, focusing on better co-ordination among departments or divisions. Phase 4 involves the top team's design of the soundest possible blueprint for the business operations of the corporation, Phase 5, carrying it out, and Phase 6, stabilizing and strengthening results. This is the Grid pattern for moving a whole company ahead toward excellence.

HAS IT WORKED?

This is the Grid pattern. What have been the results in companies that have followed it—studying the Managerial Grid and moving on into Grid Organization Development? Thousands of managers in many countries as well as the U.S. have studied the Grid and hundreds of companies are holding in-company Grid Seminars and working toward completing all the phases. Some have gone much further and extended the Grid to their wage ranks. Some firms have arranged for outside researchers from universities to evaluate their development efforts to see if there have been positive changes that can be traced specifically to Grid learning. The answer in each case is "yes."

The results have shown that Grid trained managers bring a new perspective to their work—no longer asking, "Are we doing better than last year?" or "Are we doing better than competitors?" but "What's the best we can do, not only now but in the future?" They have whole new set of optimistic *expectations* once they learn how they can manage an organization's culture instead of letting it manage them.

And they have developed new *values*—understanding the use of participation, getting commitment instead of operating by old-fashioned methods of supervision, and using experimentation and critique to learn, to change, and to improve. They are not only able to face up to conflict, but even make constructive use of disagreement, seeing it as valuable in the search for sound operational decisions.

T-Groups For Organizational Effectiveness

Chris Argyris

What causes dynamic, flexible, and enthusiastically committed executive teams to become sluggish and inflexible as time goes by? Why do they no longer enjoy the intrinsic challenge of their work, but become motivated largely by wages and executive bonus plans?

Why do executives become conformists as a company becomes older and bigger? Why do they resist saying what they truly believe—even when it is in the best interests of the company?

How is it possible to develop a top-management team that is constantly innovating and taking risks?

Is it inevitable that we get things done only when we create crises, check details, arouse fears, and penalize and reward in ways that inadvertently create "heroes" and "bums" among our executive group?

Ask managers why such problems as these exist and their answers typically will be abstract and fatalistic:

> "It's inevitable in a big business."
>
> "Because of human nature."
>
> "I'll be damned if I know, but every firm has these problems."
>
> "They are part of the bone and fabric of the company."

Statements like these *are* true. Such problems *are* ingrained into corporate life. But in recent years there has evolved a new way of helping executives develop new inner resources which enable them to mitigate these organizational

Reprinted from the *Harvard Business Review*, Vol. 42, No. 2 (March-April, 1964), 60-74, by permission of the author and the publisher.

ills. I am referring to *laboratory education*—or "sensitivity training" as it is sometimes called. Particularly in the form of "T-groups," it has rapidly become one of the most controversial educational educational experiences now available to management. Yet, as I will advocate in this article, if laboratory education is conducted competently, and if the right people attend, it can be a very powerful educational experience.

How does laboratory education remedy the problems I have mentioned? By striving to expose and modify certain values held by typical executives, values which, unless modified and added to, serve to impair interpersonal effectiveness. As Exhibit 1 explains, these values are ingrained in the pyramidal structure of the business enterprise. The exhibit summarizes several basic causes of management ineffectiveness as isolated by three studies: (1) in a large corporate division—30,000 employees, grossing $500 million per year; (2) a medium-size company—5,000 employees, grossing in excess of $50 million per year; and (3) a small company—300 employees. The results of these studies are reported in detail elsewhere.[1]

Exhibit 1. *The pyramidal values.*

There are certain values about effective human relationships that are inherent in the pyramidal structure of the business organization and which successful executives (understandably) seem to hold. Values are learned commands which, once internalized, coerce human behavior in specific directions. This is why an appreciation of these values is basic in understanding behavior.

What are these "pyradmidal" values? I would explain them this way.

1. The important human relationships—the crucial ones—are those which are related to achieving the organization's objective, i.e., getting the job done, as for example:

We are here to manufacture shoes, that is our business, those are the important human relationships; if you have anything that can influence those human relationships, fine.

2. Effectiveness in human relationships increases as behavior becomes more rational, logical, and clearly communicated; but effectiveness decreases as behavior becomes more emotional. Let me illustrate by citing a typical conversation:

"Have you ever been in a meeting where there is a lot of disagreement?"

"All the time."

"Have you ever been in a meeting when the disagreement got quite personal?"

"Well, yes I have, but not very often."

"What would you do if you were the leader of this group?"

"I would say, 'Gentlemen, let's get back to the fact,' or I would say, 'Gentlemen, let's keep personalities out of this.' If it really got bad, I would wish it were five o'clock so I could call it off, and then I would talk to the men individually."

3. Human relationships are most effectively motivated by carefully defined direction, authority, and control, as well as appropriate rewards and penalties that emphasize rational behavior and achievement of the objective.

If these are the values held by most executives, what are the consequences? To the extent that executives believe in these organizational values, the following changes have been found to happen.

(1) There is a *decrease* in receiving and giving information about executives' interpersonal impact on each other. Their interpersonal difficulties tend to be either sup-

pressed or disguised and brought up as rational, technical, intellectual problems. As a result, they may find it difficult to develop competence in dealing with feelings and interpersonal relations. There is a corresponding decrease in their ability to own up to or be responsible for their ideas, feelings, and values. Similarly there is a dropping off of experimentation and risk-taking with new ideas and values.

(2) Along with decrease in owning,* openness, risk-taking, there is an *increase* in the denial of feelings, in closeness to new ideas, and in need for stability (i.e., "don't rock the boat"). As a result, executives tend to find themselves in situations where they are not adequately aware of the human problems, where they do not solve them in such a way that they remain solved without deteriorating the problem-solving process. Thus, if we define interpersonal competence as (a) being aware of human problems, (b) solving them in such a way that they remain solved, without deteriorating the problem-solving process, these values serve to decrease interpersonal competence.

(3) As the executives' interpersonal competence decreases, conformity, mistrust, and dependence, especially on those who are in power, increase. Decision making becomes *less effective*, because people withhold many of their ideas, especially those that are innovative and risky, and organizational defenses (such as management by crisis, management by detail, and through fear) *increase*. So do such "protective" activities as "JIC" files (just in case the president asks), "information" meetings (to find out what the opposition is planning), and executive politicking.

If this analysis is valid, then we must alter executives' values if we are to make the system more effective. The question arises as to what changes can and *should* be made in these values.

But since executives are far from unknowledgeable, why have they clung to these pyramidal values? First, because they are *not necessarily wrong*. Indeed, they are a necessary part of effective human relationships. The difficulty is that alone they are not enough. By themselves they tend to lead to the above consequence. What is needed is an additional set of values for the executives to hold. Specifically there are three.

1. The important human relationships are not only those related to achieving the organization's objectives but those related to maintaining the organization's internal system and adapting to the environment, as well.

2. Human relationships increase in effectiveness as *all* the relevant behavior (rational and interpersonal) becomes conscious, discussable, and controllable. (The rationality of feelings is as crucial as that of the mind.)

3. In addition to direction, controls, and rewards and penalties, human relationships are most effectively influenced through authentic relationships, internal commitment, psychological success, and the process of confirmation. (These terms are clarified in the body of the article.)

CHANGE THROUGH EDUCATION

But how does one change an executive's values? One way is by a process of re-education. First there is an unfreezing of the old values, next the development of the new values, and finally a freezing of the new ones.

In order to begin the unfreezing process, the executives must experience the true ineffectiveness of the old values. This means they must have a "gut" experience of how incomplete the old values are. One way to achieve this is to give them a task to accomplish in situations where their power, control, and

*Defined in text, p. 173.

organizational influences are minimized. The ineffectiveness of the old values, if our analysis is correct, should then become apparent.

A second requirement of re-education arises from the fact that the overwhelming number of educational processes available (e.g., lecture, group discussion, and the like) are based on the pyramidal values. Each lecture or seminar at a university has clearly defined objectives and is hopefully staffed by a rational, articulate teacher who is capable of controlling, directing, and appropriately rewarding and penalizing the students. But, as I have just suggested, these represent some of the basic causes of the problems under study. The educator is in a bind. If he teaches by the traditional methods, he is utilizing the very values that he is holding up to be incomplete and ineffective.

To make matters more difficult, if the re-educational process is to be effective, it is necessary to create a *culture* in which the new values can be learned, practiced, and protected until the executives feel confident in using them. Such a culture would be one which is composed of people striving to develop authentic relationships and psychological success. Briefly, *authentic relationships* exist when an individual can behave in such a way as to increase his self-awareness and esteem and, at the same time, provide an opportunity for others to do the same. *Psychological success* is the experience of realistically challenging situations that tax one's capacities. Both are key components of executive competence.

The creation of a re-educational process where the unfreezing of the old values, relearning of the new values, and refreezing of the new values under primary control of the students, embedded in a culture that is rarely found in our society, is an extremely difficult task. Yet an approach to fulfilling these requirements is offered by laboratory education.

Probably because of its novelty, laboratory education has become one of the most talked about, experimented with, lauded, and questioned educational experiences for top executives. The interest of top executives has been so great that the National Training Laboratories (a nonprofit educational organization which administers most of the laboratories) has had to increase the programs manyfold in the past ten years.[2]

Any educational experience that is as novel as laboratory education is destined to be controversial. And this is good because reasoned controversy can be the basis for corrections, refinements, and expansions of the process. Research (unfortunately not enough) is being conducted under the auspices of the National Training Laboratories and at various universities such as the University of California, Case Institute of Technology, Columbia, George Washington, Harvard, M.I.T., Michigan, Texas, and Yale, to name a few.

AIMS OF PROGRAM

The first step in a laboratory program is to help the executives teach themselves as much about their behavior as possible. To do so they create their own laboratory in which to experiment. This is why the educational process has been called "laboratory education." The strategy of an experiment begins with a dilemma. A dilemma occurs when, for a given situation, there is no sound basis for selecting among alternatives, or there is no satisfactory alternative to select, or when habitual actions are no longer effective.

What do people do when confronted with a dilemma? Their immediate reaction is to try out older methods of behaving with which they are secure, or else to seek guidance from an "expert." In this way, the anxiety so invariably associated with not knowing what to do can be avoided. In the laboratory, then, the anticipated first reactions by participants to a dilemma are to try traditional ways of responding.

Only when conventional or traditional ways of dealing with a dilemma have been tried—unsuccessfully—are conditons ripe for inventive action. Now people are ready to think, to shed old notions because they have not worked, to experiment, and to explore new ways of reacting to see if they will work. The period when old behavior is being abandoned and when new behavior has yet to be invented to replace it is an "unfrozen" period, at times having some of the aspects of a crisis. It is surrounded by uncertainty and confusion.[3]

Fullest learning from the dilemma-invention situation occurs when two additional types of action are taken:

> One is feedback, the process by which members acquaint one another with their own characteristic ways of feeling and reacting in a dilemma-invention situation. Feedback aids in evaluating the consequences of actions that have been taken as a result of the dilemma situation. By "effective" feedback I mean the kind of feedback which minimizes the probability of the receiver or sender becoming defensive and maximizes his opportunity to "own" values, feelings, and attitudes. By "own" I mean being aware of and accepting responsibility for one's behavior.

> The final step in the dilemma-invention cycle is generalizing about the total sequence to get a comprehensive picture of the "common case." When this is done, people are searching to see to what extent behavior observed under laboratory conditions fits outside situations. If generalization is not attempted, the richness of dilemma-invention learning is "lost."

T FOR TRAINING

The core of most laboratories is the T (for training) group.[4] This is most difficult to describe in a few words. Basically it is a group experience designed to provide maximum possible opportunity for the individuals to expose their behavior, give and receive feedback, experiment with new behavior, and develop everlasting awareness and acceptance of self and others. The T-group, when effective, also provides individuals with the opportunity to learn the nature of effective group functioning. They are able to learn how to develop a group that achieves specific goals with minimum possible human cost.

The T-group becomes a learning experience that most closely approximates the values of the laboratory regarding the use of leadership, rewards, penalities, and information in the development of effective groups. It is in the T-group that one learns how to diagnose his own behavior, to develop effective leadership behavior and norms for decision making that truly protect the "wild duck."

ROLE OF EDUCATOR

In these groups, some of the learning comes from the educator, but most of it from the members interacting with each other. The "ground rules" the group establishes for feedback are important. With the help of the educator, the group usually comes to see the difference between providing help and attempting to control or punish a member; between analyzing and interpreting a member's adjustment (which is not helpful) and informing him of the impact it has on others. Typically, certain features of everyday group activity are blurred or removed. The educator, for example, does not provide the leadership which a group of "students" would normally expect. This produces a kind of "power vacuum" and a great deal of behavior which, in time, becomes the basis of learning.

There is no agenda, except as the group provides it. There are no norms of group operation (such as *Robert's Rules of Order*) except as the group decides to adopt them. For some time the experience is confusing, tension-laden, frustrating for most participants. But these conditions have been found to be conducive to learning. Naturally, some individuals learn a great deal, while others resist the whole process. It is rare, however, for an individual to end a two-week experience feeling that he has learned nothing.

Usually the T-group begins with the educator making explicit that it is designed to help human beings to:

> ... explore their values and their impact on others,
> ... determine if they wish to modify their old values and develop new ones,
> ... develop awareness of how groups can inhibit as well as facilitate human growth and decision making.

Thus a T-group does not begin without an objective, as far as the educator is concerned. It has a purpose, and this purpose, for the educator, is emotionally and intellectually clear.

However, the educator realizes that the purpose is, at the moment, only intellectually clear to the members. Thus, to begin, the educator will probably state that he has no specific goals in mind for the group. Moreover, he offers no specific agenda, no regulations, no rules, and so on. The group is created so its members can determine their own leadership, goals, and rules.

There is very little that is nondirective about a T-group educator's role. He is highly concerned with growth, and he acts in ways that he hopes will enhance development. He is nondirective, however, in the sense that he does not require others to accept these conditions. As one member of the T-group, he will strive sincerely and openly to help establish a culture that can lead to increased authentic relationships and interpersonal competence.

However, he realizes that he can push those in the group just so far. If he goes too far, he will fall into the trap of masterminding their education. This is a trap in which group members might like to see him fall, since it would decrease their uncomfortableness and place him in a social system similar (in values) to their own. In other words, his silence, the lack of predefined objectives, leadership, agenda, rules, and so on, are not designed to be malicious or hurt people. True, these experiences may hurt somewhat, but the hypothesis is that the pain is "in the service of growth."

At this point, let me assume that you are a member of such a T-group, so that I can tell you what you are likely to experience.

ACTION AND REACTION

At the outset you are likely to expect that the educator will lead you. This expectation is understandable for several reasons:

1. An educator in our culture tends to do precisely this.

2. Because of the newness of the situation, the members may also fear that they are not competent to deal with it effectively. They naturally turn to the educator for assistance. It is common in our culture that when one member of a group has more information than the others as to how to cope with the new, difficult situation, he is expected by the others, *if he cares for them*, to help them cope with the new situation. For example, if I am in a cave with ten other people who are lost and I know how to get out, it would be from their viewpoint the height of noncaring for me to fail to help them get out.

3. Finally, the members may turn to the educator because they have not as yet developed much trust for each other.

The educator may believe it is helpful, during the early stages of a T-group, to tell you that he understands why you feel dependent on him. But he will also add that he believes that learning can take place more effectively if you first develop an increasing sense of trust of one another and a feeling that you can learn from one another.

In my case, when I act as the educator for a T-group, I freely admit that silence is not typical of me and that I need to talk, to be active, to participate. In fact, I may even feel a mild hostility if I am in a situation in which I cannot participate in the way that I desire. Thus, anything you (members) can do to help me "unfreeze" by decreasing your dependence on me would be deeply appreciated. I add that I realize that this is not easy and that I will do my share.

Typically, the members begin to realize that the educator supports those individuals who show early signs of attempting to learn. This is especially true for those who show signs of being open, experimentally minded, and willing to take risks by exposing their behavior. How are these qualities recognized?

There are several cues that are helpful. First, there is the individual who is not highly upset by the initial ambiguity of the situation and who is ready to begin to learn. One sign of such an individual is one who can be open about the confusion that he is experiencing. He is able to own up to his feelings of being confused, without becoming hostile toward the educator or the others. Such an individual is willing to look at his and others' behavior under stress, diagnose it, and attempt to learn from it. Some of these individuals even raise questions about other members' insistence that the educator should get them out of the ambiguous situation.

Some members, on the other hand, react by insisting that the educator has created the ambiguity just to be hostile. You will find that the educator will encourage them to express their concern and hostility as well as help them to see the impact that this behavior (i.e., hostility) is having on him. There are two reasons for the educator's intervention: (1) to reinforce (with feelings) the fact that he is not callous about their feelings and that he is not consciously attempting to be hostile; and (2) to unfreeze others to explore their hostility toward him or toward each other. Such explorations can provide rich data for the group to diagnose and from which to learn.

PROBLEM OF MIMICKING

As the group continues, some members begin to realize that the educator's behavior now may serve for what it is. That is, it may be as valid a model as the educator can manifest of how he would attempt (a) to help create an effective group, and (b) to integrate himself into that group so that he becomes as fully functioning a member as possible. The model is his; he admits owning it, but he is *not* attempting to "sell" it to others or in any way to coerce them to own it.

You may wonder if viewing the educator as a source of "model behavior" would not lead you simply to *mimic* him. (In the technical literature this is discussed as "identification with the leader," or "leader modeling behavior.") Although this may be the case, we should not forget that as you begin to "unfreeze" your previous values and behavior, you will find yourself in the situation of throwing away the old and having nothing new that is concrete and workable. This tends to create states of vacillation, confusion, anxiety, ambivalence, and so on.[5] These states in turn may induce you to "hang on" to the old with even greater tenacity. To begin to substitute the new behavior for the old, you will feel a need to see (1) that you can carry out the new behavior effectively and (2) that the new behavior leads to the desired results.[6]

Under these conditions the members usually try out any bit of behavior that represents the "new." Experimentation not only is sanctioned; it is rewarded. One relatively safe way to experiment is to "try out the educator's behavior." It is at this point that the individual is mimicking. And he should feel free to mimic and *to talk about the mimicking and explore it openly.* Mimicking is helpful if you are aware of and accept the fact that you do not *own* the behavior, for the behavior with which you are experimenting is the educator's. If the educator is not anxious about the mimicking, the member may begin safely to explore the limits of the new behavior. He may also begin to see whether or not the educator's behavior is, for him, realistic.

INDIVIDUAL VERSUS GROUP

At the outset the educator tends to provide that assistance which is designed to help the members to—

> ...become aware of their present (usually) low potential for establishing authentic relationships,
> ...become more skillful in providing and receiving nonevaluative descriptive feedback,
> ...minimize their own and others' defensiveness,
> ...become increasingly able to experience and own up to their feelings.

Although interpersonal assistance is crucial, it is also important that the T-group not be limited to such interventions. After the members receive adequate feedback from one another as to their inability to create authentic relationships, they will tend to want to become more effective in their interpersonal relationships. It is at this point that they will need to learn that group structure and dynamics deeply influence the probability of increasing the authenticity of their interpersonal relations. For example:

> As soon as the members realize that they must become more open with those feelings that typically they have learned to hide, they will need to establish group norms to sanction the expression of these feelings. Also, if members find it difficult in the group to express their important

feelings, this difficulty will tend to be compounded if they feel they must "rush" their contribution and "say something quick," lest someone else take over the communication channels. Ways must be developed by which members are able to use their share of the communication channels. Also, group norms are required that sanction silence and thought, so that members do not feel coerced to say something, before they have thought it through, out of fear that they will not have an opportunity to say anything later.

An example of the interrelationship between interpersonal and group factors may be seen in the problems of developing leadership in a group. One of the recurring problems in the early stages of a T-group is the apparent need on the part of members to appoint a leader or a chairman. Typically, this need is rationalized as a group need because "without an appointed leader a group cannot be effective." For example, one member said, "Look, I think the first thing we need is to elect a leader. Without a leader we are going to get nowhere fast." Another added, "Brother, you are right. Without leadership, there is chaos. People hate to take responsibility and without a leader they will goof off."

There are several ways that your group might consider for coping with this problem, each of which provides important but different kinds of learning:

One approach is to see this as a group problem. How does leadership arise and remain helpful in a group? This level of learning is important and needs to be achieved.

Another possibility is for the group members to explore the underlying assumptions expressed by those individuals who want to appoint leaders. For example, in the case illustrated above, both men began to realize that they were assuming that people "need" appointed leadership because, if left alone, they will not tend to accept responsibility. This implies a lack of confidence in and trust of people. It also implies mistrust of the people around the table. These men were suggesting that without an appointed leader the group will flounder and become chaotic. Someone then took the initiative and suggested that their comments implied a lack of trust of the people around the table. Another individual suggested that another dimension of mistrust might also be operating. He was concerned how he would decide if he could trust the man who might be appointed as the leader. The discussion that followed illustrated to the group the double direction of the problem of trust. Not only do superiors have feelings of mistrust of subordinates, but the latter may also mistrust the former.

One of the defendants of the need for leadership then said, "Look, Mr. B. over there has been trying to say something for half an hour, and hasn't succeeded. If we had a leader, or if he himself were appointed leader temporarily, then he might get his point of view across." Several agreed with the observation. However, two added some further insightful comments. One said, "If we give Mr. B. authority, he will never have to develop his internal strength so that he can get his point across without power behind him." "Moreover," the other added, "if he does get appointed leader, the group will never have to face the problem of how it can help to create the conditions for Mr. B. to express his point of view." Thus we see that attempting to cope with the basic problems of group membership can lead to an exploration of problems of group membership as well as requirements of effectively functioning groups.

The question of trust, therefore, is a central problem in a T-group, indeed, as it is in any group organization. If this can be resolved, then the group has taken an important step in developing authentic relationships. As the degree of trust increases, "functional leadership" will tend to rise spontaneously because individuals in a climate of mutual trust will tend to delegate leadership to those who are most competent for the subject being discussed. In doing so, they also learn an important lesson about effective leadership.

Another kind of learning that usually develops clearly is that the group will not tend to become an effective task-oriented unit without having established effective means to diagnose problems, make decisions, and so on. It is as the group becomes a decision-making unit that the members can "test" the strengths and depth of their learning. The pressure and stress of decision making can help to show the degree to which authenticity is apparent rather than real. It can also provide opportunity for further learning, because the members will tend to experience new aspects of themselves as they attempt to solve problems and make decisions.

FURTHER COMPONENTS

Laboratory education has other components. I have focused in detail on T-groups because of their central role. This by no means describes the total laboratory experience. For example, laboratory education is helpful in diagnosing one's organizational problems.

Diagnosing Problems. When a laboratory program is composed of a group of executives who work in the same firm, the organizational diagnostic experiences are very important. Each executive is asked to come to the laboratory with any agenda or topic that is important to him and to the organization. During the laboratory, he is asked to lead the group in a discussion of the topic. The discussion is taped and observed by the staff (with the knowledge of the members).

Who Learns From T-Group Experiences?

People who learn in T-groups seem to possess at least three attributes:

1. A relatively strong ego that is not overwhelmed by internal conflicts.
2. Defenses which are sufficiently low to allow the individual to hear what others say to him (accurately and with minimal threat to his self), without the aid of a professional scanning and filtering system (that is, the therapist, the educator).
3. The ability to communicate thoughts and feelings with minimal distortion. In other words, the operational criterion of minimal threat is that the individual does not tend to distort greatly what he or others say, nor does he tend to condemn others or himself.

This last criterion can be used in helping to select individuals for the T-group experience. *If the individual must distort or condemn himself or others to the point that he is unable to do anything but to continue to distort the feedback that he gives and receives, then he ought not to be admitted to a T-group.*

To put this another way, T-groups, compared to therapy groups, assume a higher degree of health—not illness—that is, a higher degree of self-awareness and acceptance. This is an important point. *Individuals should not be sent to the laboratory if they are highly defensive.* Rather, the relatively healthy individuals capable of learning from others to enhance their degree of effectiveness are the kinds of individuals to be selected to attend.

Once the discussion is completed, the group members listen to themselves on the tape. They analyze the interpersonal and group dynamics that occurred in the making of the decision and study how these factors influenced their decision making. Usually, they hear how they cut each other off, did not listen, manipulated, pressured, created win-lose alternatives, and so on.

Such an analysis typically leads the executives to ask such questions as: Why do we do this to each other? What do we wish to do about it, if anything?

On the basis of my experience, executives become highly involved in answering these questions. Few hold back from citing interpersonal and organizational reasons why they feel they have to behave as they do. Most deplore the fact that time must be wasted and much energy utilized in this "windmilling" behavior. It is quite frequent for someone to ask, "But if we don't like this, why don't we do something about it?"

Under these conditions, the things learned in the laboratory are intimately interrelated with the everyday "real" problems of the organization. Where this has occurred, the members do not return to the organization with the same degree of bewilderment that executives show who have gone to laboratories full of strangers. In the latter case, it is quite common for the executive to be puzzled as to how he will use what he has learned about human competence when he returns home.[7]

Consultation Groups.   Another learning experience frequently used is to break down the participants into groups of four. Sessions are held where each individual has the opportunity both to act as a consultant giving help and as an individual receiving help. The nature of help is usually related to increasing self-awareness and self-acceptance with the view of enhancing interpersonal competence.

Lectures. As I pointed out above, research information and theories designed to help organizational learning are presented in lectures—typically at a time when it is most clearly related to the learnings that the participants are experiencing in a laboratory.

Role-Playing of "Real" Situations. As a result of the discussions at the laboratory program, many data are collected illustrating situations in which poor communications exist, objectives are not being achieved as intended, and so on. It is possible in a laboratory to role-play many of these situations, to diagnose them, to obtain new insights regarding the difficulties, as well as to develop more effective action possibilities. These can be role-played by asking the executives to play their back-home role. For other problems, however, important learnings are gained by asking the superiors to take the subordinates' role.

Developing and Testing Recommendations. In most organizations, executives acknowledge that there are long-range problems that plague an organization, but that they do not have time to analyze them thoroughly in the back-home situation (for example, effectiveness of decentralization). In a laboratory, however, time is available for them to discuss these problems thoroughly. More important, as a result of their laboratory learnings and with the assistance of the educators, they could develop new action recommendations. They could diagnose their effectiveness as a group in developing these recommendations— have they really changed; have they really enhanced their effectiveness?

Intergroup Problems. One of the central problems of organizations is the intergroup rivalries that exist among departments. If there is time in a laboratory, this topic should be dealt with. Again, it is best introduced by creating the situation where the executives compete against one another in groups under "win-lose" conditions (i.e., where only one can win and someone must lose).

CORRECTING MISUNDERSTANDINGS

Any educational activity that is as new and controversial as laboratory education is bound to have misconceptions and misunderstandings built around it. Therefore, I should like to attempt briefly to correct a few of the more commonly heard misunderstandings about laboratory education.

1. Laboratory methods in general, and T-groups in particular, are not a set of hidden, manipulative processes by which individuals can be "brain-washed" into thinking, believing, and feeling the way someone might want them to without realizing what is happening to them.

Central to a laboratory is openness and flexibility in the educational process. It is open in that it is continually described and discussed with the participants as well as constantly open to modification by them.

Along with the de-emphasis of rigidity and emphasis on flexibility, the emphasis is on teaching that kind of knowledge and helping the participants develop those kinds of skills which increase the strength and competence to question, to examine, and to modify. The objectives of a laboratory are to help an individual learn to be able to reject that which he deeply believes is inimical to his self-esteem and to his growth—and this would include, if necessary, the rejection of the laboratory experience.

2. A laboratory is not an educational process guided by a staff leader who is covertly in control and by some magic hides this fact from the participants.

A laboratory means that people come together and create a setting where (as is the case in any laboratory) they generate their own data for learning. This means that they are in control and that any behavior in the laboratory, including the staff member's, is fair game for analysis.

I should like to suggest the hypothesis that if anything is a threat to the participants, it is not the so-called covert control. The experience becomes painful when the participants begin to realize the scope and depth to which the staff is ready "to turn things over to them." Initially this is seen by many participants as the staff abdicating leadership. Those who truly learn come to realize that in doing this the staff is expressing, in a most genuine way, their faith in the potentiality of the participants to develop increasing competence in controlling more of their learning. As this awareness increases, the participants usually begin to see that their cry of "abdication of leadership" is more of a camouflage that hides from them how little they trusted each other and themselves and how overprotected they were in the past from being made to assume some responsibility for their learning.

3. The objective of laboratory education is not to suppress conflict and to get everyone to like one another.

The idea that this is the objective is so patently untrue that I am beginning to wonder if those who use it do not betray their own anxiety more than they describe what goes on in a laboratory. There is no other educational process that

I am aware of in which conflict is generated, respected, and cherished. Here conflict, hostility, and frustration become motivations for growth as well as food for learning. It is with these kinds of experiences that participants learn to take risks—the kinds of risks that can lead to an increase in self-esteem. As these experiences are "worked through" and the learnings internalized, participants soon begin to experience a deeper sense of self-awareness and acceptance. These, in turn, lead to an increased awareness and acceptance of others.

And this does *not* necessarily mean liking people. Self-acceptance means that individuals are aware of themselves and care so much about themselves that they open themselves to receiving and giving information (sometimes painful) about their impact on others and others' impact on them, so that they can grow and become more competent.

> *4. Laboratory education does not attempt to teach people to be callous, disrespectful of society, and to dislike those who live a less open life.*

If one truly begins to accept himself, he will be less inclined to condemn nongenuineness in others, but to see it for what it is, a way of coping with a nongenuine world by a person who is (understandably) a nongenuine individual.

> *5. Laboratory education is neither psychoanalysis nor intensive group therapy.*

During the past several years I have been meeting with a group of psychiatrists and clinical psychologists who are trying to differentiate between group therapy and everything else. One problem we discovered is that therapists define therapy as any change. The difficulty with this definition is that it means any change is therapy.

We have concluded that it may be best to conceive of a continuum of "more" or "less" therapy. The more the group deals with unconscious motivations, uses clinical constructs, focuses on "personal past history," and is guided in these activities by the leader, the more it is therapy. Therapy is usually characterized by high proportions of these activities because the individuals who are participating are so conflicted or defensive that they are not able to learn from each other without these activities.

In my view, a T-group is—or should be—a group that contains individuals whose internal conflicts are low enough to learn by:

> Dealing with "here and now" behavior (what is going on in the room).
>
> Using relatively nonclinical concepts and nonclinical theory.
>
> Focusing on relatively conscious (or at most preconscious) material.

Being guided increasingly less by the leader and increasingly more by each other.

Accomplishing this in a relatively (to therapy) short time (at the moment, no more than three weeks).

This does not mean that T-groups do not, at times, get into deeper and less conscious problems. They do; and, again, they vary primarily with the staff member's biases. Usually most educators warn the group members against striving to become "two bit" psychologists.

6. Laboratory education does not have to be dangerous, but it must focus on feelings.

Interpersonal problems and personal feelings exist at all levels of the organization, serving to inhibit and decrease the effectiveness of the system. Does it seem to be logical (in fact, moral) for a company to say that it is not going to focus on something that people are already experiencing and feeling? The truth is that people *do* focus on interpersonal problems every hour of the day. They simply do not do it openly.

Now for the argument that the laboratory program can hurt people and is, therefore, dangerous. The facts of life are that people are being hurt every day. I do not know of any laboratory program that did, or could, create for people as much tension as they are experiencing in their everyday work relationships.

It is true that laboratory education does require people to take risks. But does anyone know of any learning that truly leads to growth which does not involve some pain and cost? The value of laboratory education is that it keeps out the people who want to learn "cheaply" and it provides the others with control over how much they wish to learn and what they want to pay for it.

7. The objective of laboratory education is to develop effective reality-centered leaders.

Some people have expressed concern that if an executive goes through such a learning experience, he might somehow become a weak leader. Much depends on how one defines strong leadership. If strong leadership means unilateral domination and directiveness, then the individual will tend to become "weaker." But why is such leadership strong? Indeed, as I have suggested, it may be weak. Also it tends to develop subordinates who conform, fear to take risks, and are not open, and an organization that becomes increasingly rigid and has less vitality.[8]

Nor can one use the argument that directive leadership has worked and that is why it should remain. There are data to suggest that directive leadership can help an organization under certain conditions (e.g., for routine decisions and under extreme emergencies). But these conditions are limited. If directive leadership is effective beyond these relatively narrow conditions, it may be because of a self-fulfilling prophecy. Directive leadership creates dependence, submissiveness, and conformity. Under these conditions subordinates will tend to be afraid to use their initiative. Consequently, the superior will tend to fill in the vacuum with directive leadership. We now have a closed cycle.

The fact is that directive leaders who learn at a laboratory do not tend to throw away their directive skills. Rather, they seem to use directive leadership where and when it is appropriate. It cannot be emphasized too strongly that there is nothing in laboratory education which requires an individual to throw away a particular leadership pattern. The most laboratory education can do is help the individual see certain unintended consequences and costs of his leadership, and help him to develop other leadership styles *if* he wishes.

8. Change is not guaranteed as a result of attendance.

Sometimes I hear it said that laboratory education is not worthwhile, because some individuals who have attended do not change, or if they do change, it is only for a relatively short period of time.

Let me acknowledge that there is an immense gap in our knowledge about the effectiveness of a laboratory. Much research needs to be done before we know exactly what the payoff is in laboratory education. However, there are a few statements that can be made partially on the basis of research and experience and partially on the basis of theory.

One of the crucial learnings of a laboratory is related to the development of openness and trust in human relationships. These factors are not generated easily in a group. It takes much effort and risk. Those who develop trust in a group learn something very important about it. Trust cannot be issued, inspired, delegated, and transferred. It is an interpersonal factor which has to be *earned* in each relationship. This is what makes trust difficult to develop and precious to have.

Thus, it does not make very much sense to expect that suddenly an individual will act as if he can trust and can be trusted in a setting where this was never true. One executive was needled by the corporate president, who observed that he had not seen any change in the former's behavior. The executive responded: "What makes you think I feel free to change my behavior in front of you?"

This remark points up the possibility that if there is not any observable change, it could mean that the individual has not learned much. But it could also mean that he has learned a great deal, *including* the fact that he ought not to behave differently when he returns. For, it must be emphasized, laboratory education is only a partial attack on the problem of organizational effectiveness. If the changes are to become permanent, one must also change the nature of the organizational structure, managerial controls, incentive systems, reward and penalty systems, and job designs.[9]

IMPACT ON ORGANIZATION

The impact of laboratory education on the effectivenss of an organization is extremely difficult to isolate and measure.[10] Organizations are so complex, and their activities influenced by so many factors, that it is difficult to be precise in specifying the causes of the impact.

In one study that I conducted of the 20 top executives of a large corporate division, I did find a significant shift on the part of the experimental group toward a set of values that encouraged the executives to handle feelings and emotions, deal with problems of group maintenance, and develop greater feelings of responsibility on the part of their subordinates for the effectiveness of the organization. This shift is quantified in Exhibit 2.

Exhibit 2.   *Before and after values of 11 executives who experienced laboratory education*

In an administrative situation, whenever possible . . .	Before T-group	Six months after
1a. The leader should translate interpersonal problems into rational intellective ones	100%	10%
1b. The leader should deal with the interpersonal problems	0	81
2a. The leader should stop emotional disagreement by redefining the rational purpose of the meeting	90	10
2b. The leader should bring out emotional disagreements and help them to be understood and resolved	6	81
3a. When strong emotions erupt, the leader should require himself and others to leave them alone and not deal with them	100	18
3b. When strong emotions erupt, the leader should require himself and offer others the opportunity to deal with them	0	82
4a. If it becomes necessary to deal with feelings, the leader should do it even if he feels he is not the best qualified	100	9
4b. The leader should encourage the most competent members	0	90
5a. The leader is completely responsible for keeping the group "on the track" during a meeting	100	0
5b. The group members as well as the leader are responsible for keeping the group "on the track"	0	100

As the exhibit shows, the impact of laboratory education continued at a high level for a period in excess of six months. However, during the tenth month a fade-out began to appear. *This was studied and data were obtained to suggest that the executives had not lost their capacity to behave in a more open and trustful manner, but they had to suppress some of this learning because the corporate president and the other divisional presidents, who were not participants in the laboratory, did not understand them.*

This finding points up two important problems. Change is not going to be effective and permanent *until the total organization* accepts the new values. Also, effective change does *not* mean that the executives must lose their capacity to behave according to the pyramidal values. They do so whenever it is necessary. However, now they have an additional way to behave, and they use it whenever possible. They report that irrespective of the problem of acceptance by others, they find the pyramidal values are effective when they are dealing primarily with *routine, programed* decisions. The new values and manner of leadership seem to be best suited for decisions that are *unprogramed, innovative,* and require high commitment.

It is important to emphasize that laboratory education does *not* tell anyone what type of leadership to select. It does not urge him always to be more "democratic" or "collaborative." A successful laboratory helps the executives realize the unintended costs of the "old," develop "new" leadership behavior and philosophies, and become competent in utilizing whatever leadership style is appropriate in a given situation. A laboratory helps an individual increase his repertory of leadership skills and his freedom to choose how he will behave. If it coerces the executive, it is for him to become more *reality-centered.*

Another way of describing the impact of a laboratory program on an organization is for me to offer you excerpts from a tape of a meeting where the executives discussed the difficulties as well as successes that they were having 30 days after the program. The first part of the tape contains a discussion of examples of concrete changes which the members felt were a result of the laboratory. Here is a sample of the changes reported:

1. Executives reported the development of a new program for certain pricing policies that could not be agreed upon before, and laid part of the success to their new ability to sense feelings.

2. One executive stated, "We are consciously trying to change our memos. For example, we found a way to decrease the 'win-lose' feelings and 'rivalries.' "

3. The personnel director reported a distinct improvement in the sensitivity of the line managers to the importance of personnel problems, which before the laboratory seemed to have a second-class status. He said he was especially pleased with the line executives' new awareness of the complexity of personnel problems and their willingness to spend more time on solving them.

The rest of the tape is excerpted and presented in Exhibit 3.

Exhibit 3. *Discussion of attitude changes by T-group members.*

The excerpt presented here mirrors the tone of the entire meeting. I have not purposely selected only that section in which the men praised the laboratory. If the men had criticized the laboratory, such criticism would have been included. As you may see, the researcher actually pushed the group for more negative comments.

Except for minor editing, these are direct quotes:

No. 4 [after reporting that his superior, a member of the experimental group, had made a decision which should have been left to him]: I was really fuming. I was angry as hell. I walked into his office and I said to myself, "No matter what the hell happens, I'm going to tell him that he cannot do that any more." Well, I told him so. I was quite emotional. You know it floored me. He looked at me and said, "You're right; I made a mistake, and I won't do that again." Well I just don't think he would have done that before.

No. 7: The most important factor in motivating people is not what you say or do; it's giving a person the opportunity to express his views and the feeling that one is seriously interested in his views. I do much less selling but it sure takes longer.

No. 2: I've had a problem. I now have a greater need for feedback than before, and I find it difficult to get. The discussion on internal commitment made much sense to me, and I try to see if I can create conditions for it.

The thing that bothers me is that I try to handle it correctly, but I don't get feedback or cues as to how well I'm doing, as I used to at the lab. The meeting is over, and you don't know whether you've scored or not. So after each meeting I've got 10 question marks. The things that before were never questions are now question marks.

You don't get feedback. You ask for something and they respond, "I know what you're trying to do." They think I've something up my sleeve. All I want is to get feedback. It was obvious to me they were all waiting for me to make the decision. But I wanted them to make it. This was their baby, and I wanted them to make it. Two days later they made it. Fine, in this case I got feedback. The point was that their decision was a severe reversal, and I realize it was difficult for them to make. But they made it. Before, I simply would have pointed out the facts, and they would have "agreed" with the reversal, but down deep

inside they would have felt that they could have continued on. As it is now, it's their decision. I think they now have a greater sense of internal commitment. People are now freer to disagree.

No. 11: My list of decisions to be made is longer. I am hoping that they will make some decisions. I now know how much they wait for me.

No. 11 [after telling how he wrote a note which in effect damned No. 2 and maintained his own correctness, then reread it and realized how defensive it was]: Before I wouldn't have even seen this.

No. 2: One of our most difficult jobs will be to write our feelings and to write in such a way that others can express their feelings.

No. 3: I have some difficulties in evaluating this program. What have we gotten out of this? What are we able to verbalize about what we got out of this? Do others of you have difficulty in verbalizing it?

No. 2: I have the same difficulty. I have been totally ineffective describing the experience.

No. 8: Each time I try I give a different answer.

No. 1: I don't have too much difficulty. One thing that I am certain of is that I see people more as total human beings. I see aspects of them that I had never seen before.

No. 9: I'm frustrated because I now realize the importance of face-to-face communication. I'm so far from the general managers that it is not so hot. Has anyone tried to write memos that really get feelings brought out?

I find myself questioning much more than I ever did before. I have a more questioning attitude. I take into account more factors.

No. 4: We've been talking about things as if we've slowed down a bit. We haven't. For example, remember you [No. 1] and I had a problem? I'm sure Arden House was very helpful. If I hadn't been there, my reaction to you would have been different. I would have fought you for hours.

No. 1: I know we can talk to each other more clearly. It's not a conscious way. It's spontaneous.

No. 3: I have to agree we can make some decisions much faster. For example, with No. 2 I simply used to shut up. But now I can be more open. Before the laboratory, if I had an intuitive feeling that something was wrong, but I wasn't sure, I'd keep quiet until things got so bad that then I'd have a case to go to the boss. Now I feel freer to talk about it sooner and with No. 2.

I now feel that we are going to say exactly how we feel to anyone. You [the president], for example, don't have to worry, and, therefore, question, probe, and draw us out. President: Yes, and today I found No. 1, who told me that he simply would not agree with me. And I said to myself, "God bless you. He really is open now."

No. 1: I agree. I would not have expressed this feeling before being in this group. It's obvious that one should but I didn't.

[No. 2 and No. 1 show real insight into how they are being manipulated by people outside and above the group. They are much more aware of the manipulative process. "This kind of manipulation is dynamite. It burns me up."]

No. 1: Yes, it's really horrible to see it and not be able to do anything about it.

No. 7: In this case it seems to me you've got to really hit hard, because you're dealing with an untrained man [laughter].... I think I now have a new understanding of decision making. I am now more keenly aware of the importance of getting a consensus so that the *implementation* is effective. I am not trying to say that I do this in every meeting. But I do strive more to give opportunity for consensus.

No. 1: One of the problems that I feel is that the "initiated" get confused so they don't play the game correctly. Sometimes I feel walked upon, so I get sore. This is difficult. [Many others expressed agreement.]

No. 6: Does it help to say, "I trust you?" I think it does.

No. 11: For example, No. 2, you went to a meeting where you admitted you had made

a mistake. Boy, you should have heard the reaction. Boy, Mr. —— admitted a mistake. Well, wonderful; it helped to get these guys to really feel motivated to get the job done.

No. 9: Yes, I heard that many took on a deeper feeling of responsibility to get the program on the right track.

No. 7: I'd like to come back to what No. 6 said. I used to say to people that I trusted them, that I was honest, and so on. But now I wonder if people really believe me, or if they don't begin to think if I'm not covering that I'm not honest.

No. 3: Another example which I am now aware of is the typical way we write memos. We start off: "I have confidence in your judgment to handle this question," and so on. Few more paragraphs. Then fifth paragraph reads: "Please confirm by return mail exactly what you have done and what controls have been set up."

No. 2: I agree. We do an awful lot to control people. Although I think that we're trying.

[No. 7 gave examples of how he stopped making a few phone calls to exert pressure. Others agreed.]

The researcher: Aren't there negative comments?

No. 11: We have one man who has chosen not to be here. I wonder why?

No. 3: Well, really, to me that is a sign of health in the group. He feels he would still be accepted even if he didn't come. It certainly would be easy for him to come and just sit here.

No. 1: Yes, he wouldn't go to the trouble of avoiding a meeting that you didn't think was important.

No. 3: The only negative that I can think is: "What can you tell me that actually increases effectiveness?" I am not sure, but I must agree that there is a whale of a different climate.

No. 7: Well, I'd like to develop a list of things that we feel we have gotten out of this program so far. How do others of you feel? [All agreed, "Let's try."]

[All group members reporting they reached the following conclusions.]

(a) All of us begin to see ourselves as others see us . . . a real plus.

(b) A degree of greater confidence in oneself in meetings and in interviews. Beginning to be more comfortable with self.

(c) Greater confidence in associates. We feel more secure that you're telling what you think. . . . Greater feeling of freedom of expression to say what you really think.

(d) Individuals have a greater understanding and appreciation of viewpoint of associates.

(e) Greater appreciation of the opposite viewpoint.

(f) An awareness of what we do and others do that inhibits discussion.

(g) More effective use of our resources . . . getting more from them, and they feel this . . . patient to listen more.

(h) Meetings do not take longer and implementation is more effective. Internal commitment is greater.

(i) We have had a great realization that being only task-oriented, we will not get the best results. We must not forget worrying about the organization and the people.

(j) We get more irritated to infringement of our jobs and unique contributions.

(k) Fewer homemade crises.

No. 6: One of the difficult things about the list is that when you look at it, you wake up to the fact that you haven't really been using these principles. When you tell someone else who doesn't realize the gap between knowing something and actually doing it, he doesn't realize.

No. 7: But I think I really did learn and do care. Now when I think what I used to do, because that was the way. Today I realize that I could have had three times as much if I had known what I know now."

CONCLUSION

While I do not hold up laboratory education as a panacea to remedy all organizational problems, I do feel that six conclusions can fairly be drawn:

1. Laboratory education is a very promising educational process. Experience to date suggests that it can help some organizations to *begin* to overcome some of their problems.

2. Laboratory education is *not* a panacea, nor is it a process that can help every organization. Furthermore, it must be followed by changes in the organization, its policies, managerial controls, and even technology. Not all organizations can profit from it; nor do all organizations need similar amounts of it. All these factors should be carefully explored before becoming involved.

3. Not all laboratory programs are alike. Some focus more on interpersonal learning, some on intellectual problem solving, some on small groups, some on intergroups, and some on varying combinations of all of these. Again a careful diagnosis can help one to choose the right combination for the organization, as well as the appropriate educators. Nor are all laboratory programs equally effective. The competence of the educators can vary tremendously, as well as the receptivity of those who attend. The best thing to do is to attempt to attend a laboratory program conducted by competent professionals.

4. Openness, trust, commitment, and risk-taking grow only where the climate is supportive. A one-shot program, even at its best, can only begin

the process of unfreezing the executive system. For optimum results, repeat or "booster" programs will be necessary.

5. Although I personally believe that a laboratory program with the "natural" or actual working groups has the greatest probable payoff, it also has the greatest risk. However, one does not have to begin the process this way. There are many different ways to "seed" an organization, hoping to develop increasing trust and risk-taking. The way that will be most effective can best be ascertained by appropriate study of the executive system.

6. Finally, if you ever talk to an individual who has had a successful experience in a laboratory, you may wonder why he seems to have difficulty in describing the experience. I know I still have difficulty describing this type of education to a person who is a stranger to it.

I am beginning to realize that one reason for the difficulty in communication is that the meaningfulness of a laboratory experience varies enormously with each person. Some learn much; some learn little. I find that my learning has varied with the success of the laboratory. Some can hardly wait until it is over; others wish that it would never end. Anyone who understands a laboratory realizes that all these feelings can be real and valid. Consequently, to attempts to describe a laboratory (especially a T-group) to an individual who has never experienced one is difficult because he may be one of those persons who would not have enjoyed the process at all. Therefore, an enthusiastic description may sound hollow.

Another reason why it is difficult to communicate is that the same words can have different meanings to different people. Thus one of the learnings consistently reported by people who have completed a laboratory is that the trust, openness, leveling, risk-taking (and others) take on a new meaning—a meaning that they had not appreciated before the laboratory. This makes it difficult for a person who found laboratory education meaningful to describe it to another. He may want very much to communicate the new meanings of trust, risk-taking, and so on, but he knows, from his own skepticism before the laboratory, that this is a difficult undertaking and that it is not likely to succeed.

The point to all this is that the results of laboratory education are always individualistic; they reflect the individual and the organization. The best way to learn about it is to experience it for one's self.

NOTES

1. Chris Argyris, *Interpersonal Competence and Organizational Effectiveness* (Homewood, Illinois: Richard D. Irwin, Inc., 1962); *Understanding Organizational Behavior* (Homewood, Illinois: The Dorsey Press, Inc., 1960); and *Explorations in Human Compe-*

tence (manuscript, Department of Industrial Administration, Yale University, New Haven, 1964).

2. For information regarding the training laboratories that are available, one may write to Dr. Leland P. Bradford, National Training Laboratories, National Education Association, 1201 16th Street, Northwest, Washington, D.C. 20006.

3. See Robert K. Blake and Jane S. Mouton, *The Managerial Grid* (Houston, Texas: Gulf Publishing Co., 1963).

4. For a detailed summary of research related to laboratory education, see Dorothy Stock, "A Summary of Research on Training Groups," in *T-Group Theory and Laboratory Method; Innovation in Education,* edited by Leland Bradford, Kenneth Beene, and Jack Gibb (New York: John Wiley and Sons, Inc., 1964).

5. Roger Barker, Beatrice A. Wright, and Mollie R. Gonick, "Adjustment to Physical Handicap and Illness," *Social Science Research Council Bulletin 55,* 1946, pp. 19-54.

6. Ronald Lippitt, Jeanne Watson, and Bruce Westley, *The Dynamics of Planned Change* (New York: Harcourt, Brace & World, Inc., 1958).

7. For an example, see Argyris, *Interpersonal Competence and Organizational Effectiveness,* op. cit., Chapter 9.

8. *Ibid.*

9. For a more theoretical discussion of this matter, see Chris Argyris, *Integrating the Individual and the Organization* (New York: John Wiley and Sons, Inc., 1964).

10. Robert K. Blake and Jane S. Mouton, "Toward Achieving Organization Excellence," in *Organizational Change,* edited by Warren Bennis (New York: John Wiley and Sons, Inc., 1964). As this article went to press, I read an excellent manuscript of a speech evaluating the effectiveness of laboratory education, "The Effect of Laboratory Education Upon Individual Behavior," given by Douglas R. Bunker before the Industrial Relations Research Association in Boston on December 28, 1963.

ADDITIONAL READINGS FOR CHAPTER 6

Argyris, Chris, INTERPERSONAL COMPETENCE AND ORGANIZATIONAL EFFEC-
TIVENESS (Homewood, Illinois: Richard D. Irwin, Inc., and The Dorsey Press, 1962).

——————————, ORGANIZATION AND INNOVATION (Homewood, Illinois: Richard D. Irwin, Inc., and The Dorsey Press, 1965).

Blake, Robert R. and Jane S. Mouton, THE MANAGERIAL GRID (Houston, Texas: Gulf Publishing Company, 1964).

——————————, CORPORATE EXCELLENCE THROUGH GRID ORGANIZATION DEVELOPMENT (Houston, Texas: Gulf Publishing Company, 1968).

——————————, BUILDING A DYNAMIC CORPORATION THROUGH GRID ORGANIZATION DEVELOPMENT (Reading, Massachusetts: Addison-Wesley Publishing Company, 1969).

Bennis, Warren G., CHANGING ORGANIZATIONS (New York: McGraw-Hill Book Company, 1966).

——————————, ORGANIZATION DEVELOPMENT: ITS NATURE, ORIGINS, AND PROSPECTS (Reading, Massachusetts: Addison-Wesley Publishing Company, 1969).

Lippitt, Gordon L., ORGANIZATION RENEWAL (New York: Appleton-Century-Crofts, 1969).